Harcourt
Health and Fitness

 **Harcourt**
SCHOOL PUBLISHERS

Orlando • Austin • New York • San Diego • Toronto • London

Visit *The Learning Site!*
www.harcourtschool.com

CONSULTING AUTHORS

Lisa Bunting, M.Ed.
Physical Education Teacher
Katy Independent School District
Houston, Texas

Thomas M. Fleming, Ph.D.
Health and Physical Education
    Consultant
Lenoir City, Tennessee

Charlie Gibbons, Ed.D.
Director, Youth and School Age
    Programs
Maxwell Air Force Base, Alabama
Former Adjunct Professor,
    Alabama State University
Health, Physical Education and
    Dance Department
Montgomery, Alabama

Jan Marie Ozias, Ph.D., R.N.
Former Director, Texas Diabetes
    Council; and Consultant,
    School Health Programs
Austin, Texas

Carl Anthony Stockton, Ph.D.
Dean, School of Education
The University of Texas at
    Brownsville and Texas
    Southmost College
Brownsville, Texas
Former Department Chair and
    Professor of Health Education
Department of Health and
    Applied Human Sciences
The University of North Carolina
    at Wilmington
Wilmington, North Carolina

Printed in the United States of America

ISBN 13: 978-0-15-355123-9

ISBN 10: 0-15-355123-2

1 2 3 4 5 6 7 8 9 10   032   15 14 13 12 11 10 09 08 07 06

Chapters

Contents

CHAPTER 1

Your Growing Body 2

CHAPTER 2

Caring for Your Body 24

DANGER!

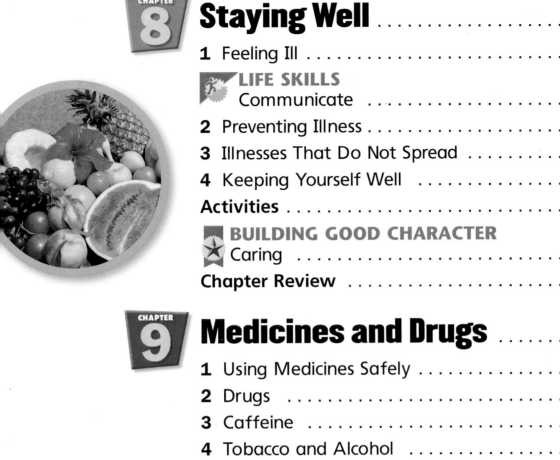

Caring for Your Neighborhood

Reading in Health Handbook

Health and Safety Handbook

Glossary

Index

Why should you learn about health?

You can do many things to help yourself stay healthy and fit. You can also avoid doing things that will harm you. If you know ways to stay safe and healthy and do these things, you can help yourself have good health.

Staying active

Getting enough rest

Eating right

Keeping clean

Staying away from alcohol, tobacco, and other drugs

Having good relationships with family and friends

Dealing with feelings in good ways

Why should you learn about life skills?

Being healthy and fit doesn't come from just knowing facts. You also have to think about these facts. You have to know how to use them every day.

These are some important life skills for you to have:

Communicating
Sharing ideas, needs, and feelings

Making Decisions
Choosing the best thing to do

Managing Stress
Finding ways to help yourself relax

Refusing
Saying NO to things that can hurt you

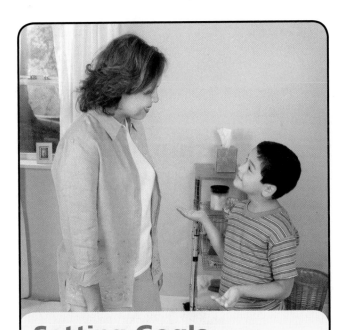

Setting Goals
Deciding on ways to improve your health and fitness

Resolving Conflicts
Finding ways to solve problems that let both sides win

Whenever you see ![LIFE SKILLS] in this book, you can learn more about using life skills.

Why should you learn about good character?

Having good character is also an important part of having good health. When you have good character, you have good relationships with others. You can make good decisions about your health and fitness.

These are some important character traits:

Caring
Showing kindness to friends, family, and others

Fairness
Treating others equally, playing by the rules, and being a good sport

Citizenship
Having pride in your school and community and obeying rules and laws

Respect

Being considerate of yourself and others

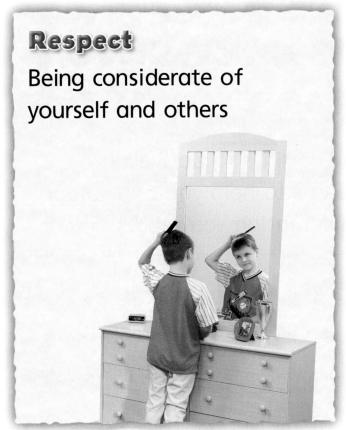

Responsibility

Doing what you are supposed to do and showing self-control

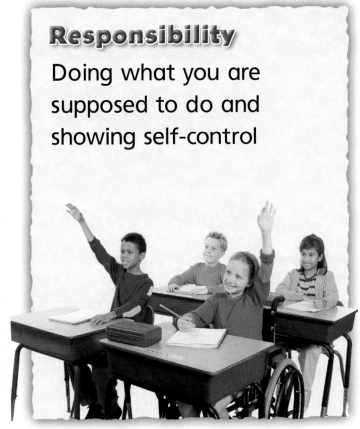

Honesty

Telling the truth so others can trust you

Whenever you see **Building Good Character** in this book, you can learn more about building good character.

What are ways to be a successful reader?

You need good reading skills to do well in school. Here are some tips to help you understand, remember, and use information you read.

Reading Tip

This section tells you what the lesson is about.

Reading Tip

Vocabulary words are listed at the beginning of the lesson. They are also highlighted and defined when they are first used.

LESSON 3 **Caffeine**

Lesson Focus
Caffeine is a drug that can harm you.

Vocabulary
caffeine
habit

Caffeine is a drug. It changes the way the body works. Tea, coffee, chocolate, and soft drinks may contain caffeine.

Some products have caffeine even though it is not listed on the label. Others have the caffeine taken out. These products are "caffeine free."

174

TEA

TEA

COFFEE

COCOA

COLA

Chocolate CANDY

Whenever you see in this book, you can learn more about using reading skills.

Some people have a habit of using caffeine. A **habit** is something a person does often. Someone with a caffeine habit drinks caffeine drinks instead of more healthful drinks. Too much caffeine can make your heart beat fast and make you feel nervous. Caffeine can make it hard to sleep.

Reading Tip

Answer these questions to check how well you understood the lesson.

Review

1 **Vocabulary** What is **caffeine**, and what foods and drinks contain it?

2 How can having caffeine become a habit?

3 Write about why you might choose foods and drinks without caffeine.

175

Throughout **Harcourt Health and Fitness,** you will be able to learn new ideas and skills that will lead to good health.

Your Growing Body

Reading Skill

Sequence

When you sequence things, you put them in the order in which they happen.

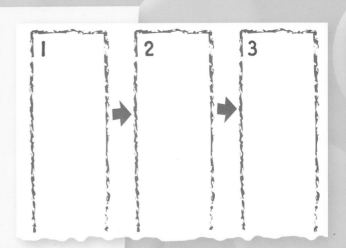

Health Graph

Number of Jumping Jacks in 15 Seconds

Children

Maria

Devon

MiWon

0 1 2 3 4 5 6 7 8 9 10

Number of Jumping Jacks

Daily Physical Activity

You should exercise every day. It helps you take care of your growing body and its many parts.

Be Active!

Use **Saucy Salsa** on Track 1.

You Are Growing

Growing means getting bigger and older. Animals grow and change. A puppy grows into an adult dog. A kitten grows into a cat. A bird comes out of an egg. It grows into an adult bird.

People also grow and change. You were a baby once. Now you are a child. You will grow to be a teenager. Then you will become an adult. You will keep getting older.

Your body changes as you grow. You get taller and heavier. Adults do not get taller, but their bodies still change. Their skin gets wrinkles. Their hair may change color.

Growing brings many changes. You will get bigger and older. But you will still be you.

Review

1. **Vocabulary** How do you know you are **growing**?

2. Draw pictures to show what you look like now and what you may look like as an adult.

3.  Write these words in order from youngest to oldest—teenager, child, adult, baby.

Your Skeletal and Muscular Systems

Lesson Focus
Your bones and muscles hold up your body and help it move.

Vocabulary
skeletal system
skull
spine
muscular system
muscles

Your bones make up your **skeletal system**, or skeleton. Your skeletal system holds up your body and gives it shape.

Some bones protect parts inside your body.

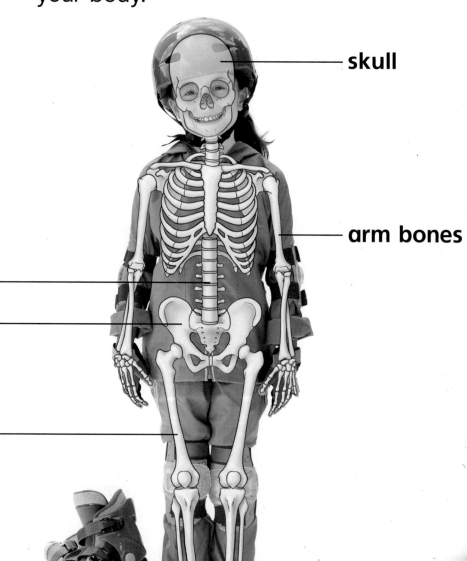

skull

arm bones

spine (backbone)

hip bones

leg bones

Skull

The bones in your head and face make up your **skull**. Your skull protects your brain.

Spine

Your **spine**, or backbone, is made up of many small bones. Your spine helps you sit, stand, and move.

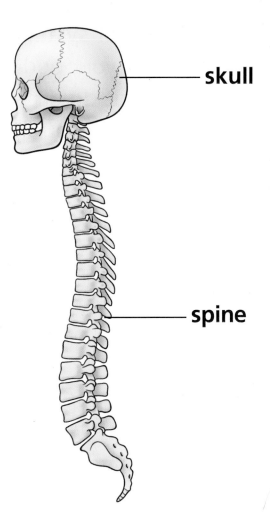

skull

spine

Caring for Your Skeletal System

► Wear a helmet and other safety gear when you ride your bike or play sports.

► Eat foods that help keep bones hard and strong.

► Exercise to keep your bones healthy and strong.

Your **muscular system** is made up of the muscles in your body. **Muscles** are body parts that do different jobs. Some muscles help hold you up. Other muscles pull on your bones to move them.

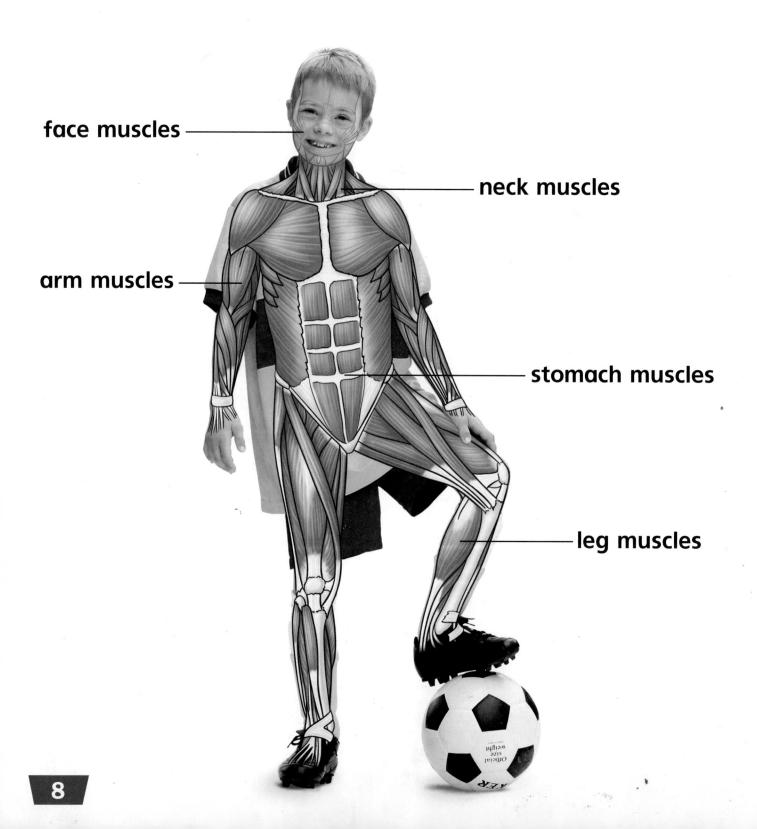

face muscles

neck muscles

arm muscles

stomach muscles

leg muscles

Caring for Your Muscular System

► Exercise to keep your muscles strong.

► Stretch your muscles before you exercise.

Review

1 Vocabulary What does your **skull** protect?

2 What do your muscles do?

3 Draw pictures to show ways you used your muscles today.

Your Digestive System

Lesson Focus
Your digestive system helps your body get energy from food.

Vocabulary
digestive system
stomach

The **digestive system** is made up of the mouth, the stomach, and other body parts. Your digestive system helps your body use food to get energy.

Caring for Your Digestive System

► Eat vegetables and fruits. They help other foods move through your digestive system.

► Eat slowly. Chew your food well.

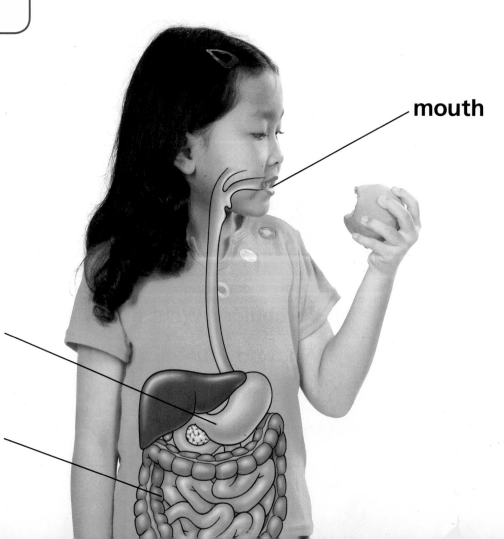

mouth

stomach

intestines

Mouth

You use different parts of your mouth to eat. Your teeth bite and chew your food. Your tongue pushes the food around your mouth so you can chew it. Then your tongue pushes the food into your throat.

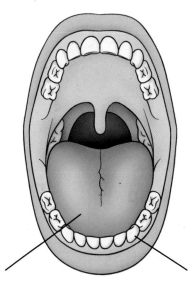

tongue · teeth

Stomach

The food moves from your throat to your stomach. Muscles in your **stomach** mix special juices with the food. The food becomes a thick liquid. Then the liquid moves from your stomach to other parts of your body.

Review

1 Vocabulary What does your **digestive system** do?

2 How do your teeth help you eat?

3 Write about what your tongue does.

Respiratory and Circulatory Systems

Lesson Focus

Your lungs help you breathe. Your heart pumps blood through your body.

Vocabulary

respiratory system

lungs

circulatory system

heart

blood vessels

The **respiratory system** is made up of the mouth, the nose, the lungs, and other parts of the body. Your respiratory system lets you breathe. Air goes in and out of your body through your mouth and nose.

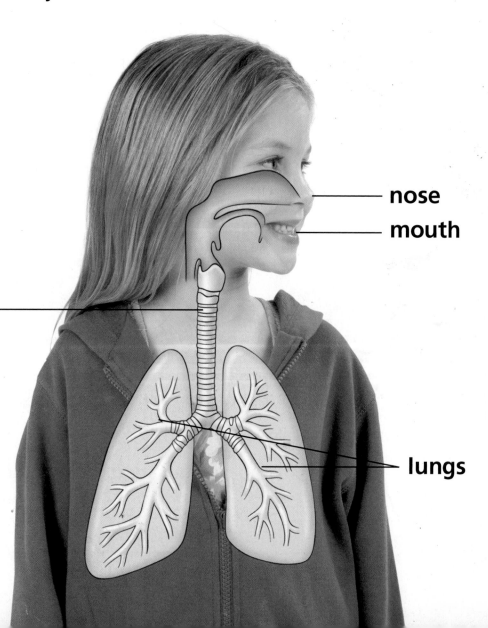

nose

mouth

trachea

lungs

Lungs

When you breathe in, air moves into your **lungs**. They fill with air and get larger. When you breathe out, air leaves your lungs and they get smaller.

Your lungs take oxygen from the air. This oxygen helps your body work.

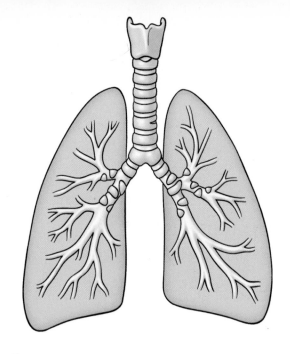

Caring for Your Respiratory System

► Exercise enough to make you breathe harder. Breathing harder makes your lungs stronger.

► Never put anything into your nose. Air goes into and out of your body through your nose.

The **circulatory system** is made up of the heart and blood vessels. Your **heart** is a muscle. It pumps, or pushes, blood through your blood vessels. **Blood vessels** are tubes that carry blood from your heart to every part of your body. The blood holds oxygen from your lungs. In this way, your whole body gets the oxygen it needs.

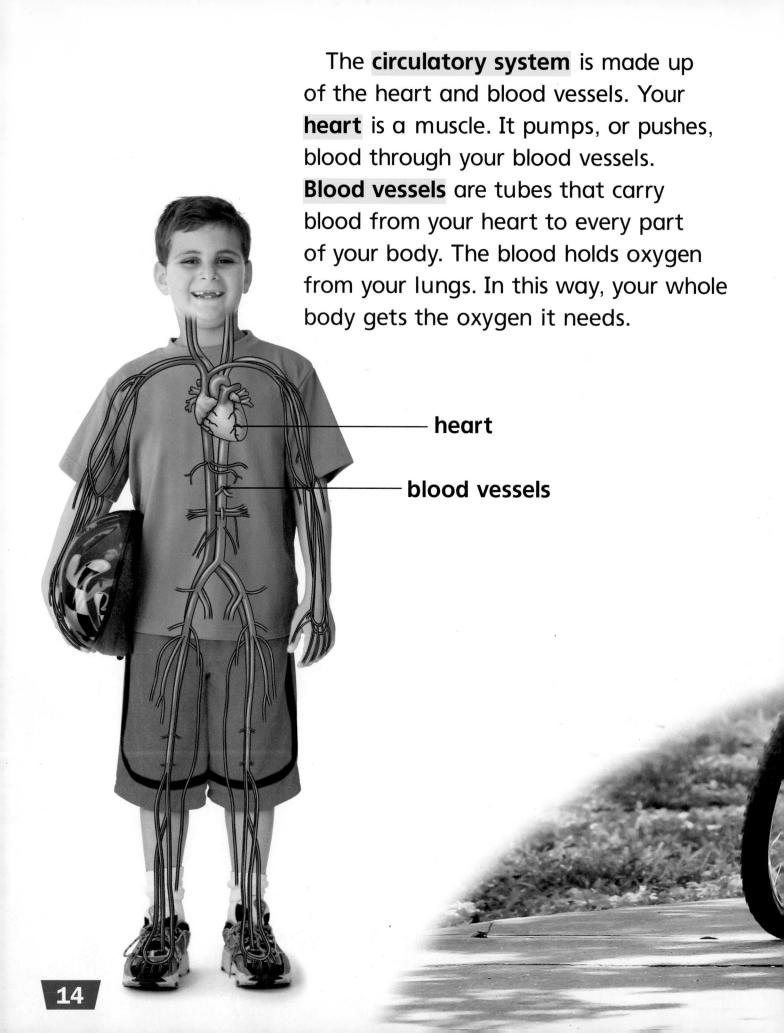

heart

blood vessels

Heart

Your heart is always pumping. Your heartbeat is the sound of your heart pumping.

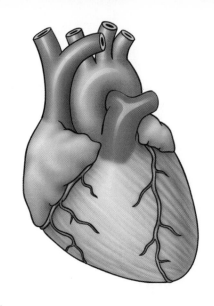

Caring for Your Circulatory System

► Exercise. Your heart muscle gets stronger when it works harder.

► Eat foods that help your blood carry oxygen. Meat and green leafy vegetables do this.

Review

1. **Vocabulary** What does your **heart** do?

2. Where does air enter your body?

3. Write about why it is important for blood to move all through your body.

15

Your Nervous System

Your nerves and brain are parts of your **nervous system**. Your **brain** gets information from your five senses— sight, hearing, touch, smell, and taste. Then your brain sends out messages through your nerves to tell your body what to do.

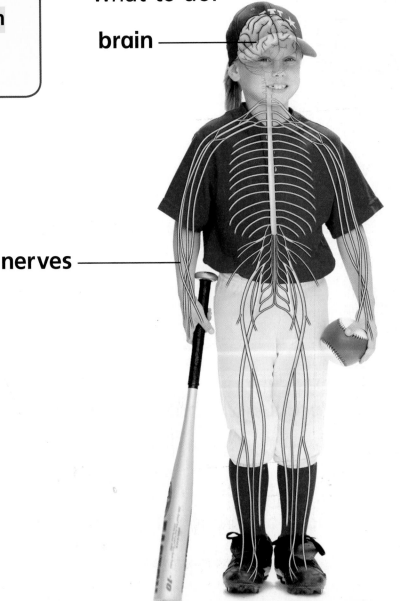

brain

nerves

Brain

Your brain controls all the other parts of your body. Your brain also lets you think, remember, and have feelings.

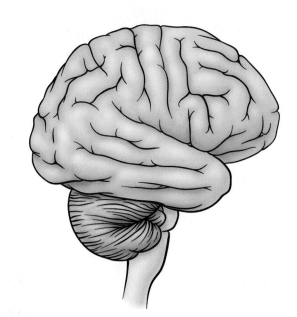

Caring for Your Nervous System

► Wear a helmet to protect your head and brain when you ride a bike or play sports.

► Get plenty of sleep. Sleep lets your brain rest.

Review

1 **Vocabulary** What parts of your body make up your **nervous system**?

2 What are the five senses?

3 Write about three things your brain does.

Set Goals

A **goal** is something you want to work toward, or reach. You can set goals for yourself. You can reach your goals. What health goal do you want to reach?

1 Set a goal.

Lea's goal is to keep her body healthy. Lea knows that exercise will help her reach her goal.

2 Make a plan to meet the goal.

Lea and her mom talk about Lea's exercise plan. Each day, Lea will swim or do chores.

3 Work toward the goal.

Lea makes a chart. Each day she swims or does chores. Then Lea marks the chart.

4 Ask yourself how you are doing.

Lea follows her exercise plan. She thinks she is doing well. Lea knows she can reach her goal.

Problem Solving

Use the steps to solve this problem.

You want to keep your body healthy. What can you do to meet this goal? How can you keep track of what you do and how you are doing?

ACTIVITIES

Math

Activity Tally Table

How many children chose running?

Which exercise was chosen by the most children?

Make a tally table of some ways your classmates stay active.

Ways We Stay Active	
biking	‖‖‖
running	‖‖
walking	‖
playing	‖‖‖

Writing

Ways You Are Changing

Think about ways you are changing as you grow. Write about some of these changes. You may want to draw pictures to go with your sentences.

Grocery Store

How I Help Grandpa

I help at the store.

GO ONLINE For more activities, visit The Learning Site.
www.harcourtschool.com/health

Caring

Being a Good Friend

As you grow, you will make new friends. You are a good friend when you are caring toward someone. A **caring** friend is thoughtful and kind. There are many ways to be a caring friend. Help your friends. Think about their feelings. Share with them. Listen carefully when they speak. Care about others who are different from you. Include them in your activities. They can be your friends, too.

How are these friends showing they care about each other?

Activity

Work with a partner. Act out some ways you can be a good friend.

21

Chapter Review

Use Health Words

Tell which picture goes with the word.

1. lungs
2. heart
3. brain
4. muscle

a.

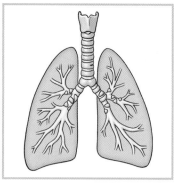

b.

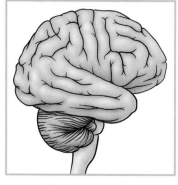

c.

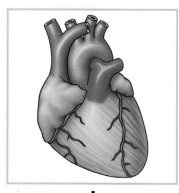

d.

Reading Skill

5. Sequence these words–teenager, baby, child.
   Write a sentence for each word.

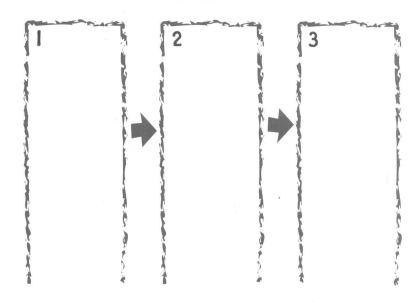

Use Life Skills

Look at the picture. Then answer the questions.

6 What is Lea doing to help her set a goal?

7 How can you set and reach health goals?

Write About It

8 Write a list of ways you can care for your body as you grow.

I can care for my body.

Reading Skill

Make Predictions

When you make a prediction, you tell what you think will happen next.

> Prediction
>
> What Happened

Health Graph

Times We Wash Our Hands

Chun

Rita

Carlos

Children

0 1 2 3 4 5 6

Number of Times

Daily Physical Activity

You should care for your body to help it stay healthy. Exercise helps it stay healthy, too.

Be Active!

Use **Get On Board** on Track 2.

Caring for Skin, Nails, and Hair

Lesson Focus
Caring for your skin, nails, and hair helps keep your body healthy.

Vocabulary
sunburn
sunscreen
germs

You need to care for your skin. One way is to protect it from sunburn. **Sunburn** is a burn from the sun. It hurts, and it harms your skin.

The sun is very strong. It can burn you even on a cloudy day. It can burn you through your clothes and your hair.

Follow these tips to protect your skin.

► Put on sunscreen before you go outside. **Sunscreen** is a product that protects skin from the sun.

► Put on more sunscreen after you swim or exercise.

► Wear a hat that protects your head and shades your face.

► Wear clothes that protect your skin.

► Stay out of the sun from 10:00 in the morning until 4:00 in the afternoon.

You can also care for your skin by keeping it clean. Washing with soap and warm water removes germs. **Germs** are tiny things that can make you ill. Your hands pick up many germs. Be sure to wash your hands at these times.

- ► after coughing or blowing your nose
- ► after using the restroom
- ► after touching an animal
- ► after playing outside
- ► before touching or eating food

Take baths or showers to clean your body. Use shampoo to clean your hair. Use soap to clean your skin and nails.

Do not bite your nails. You could hurt the skin around your nails. Trim your nails instead.

Review

1. **Vocabulary** What are **germs**?

2. Name three times when you should wash your hands.

3. Draw and label two things you should do to protect your skin when you are outside.

Head Lice

Lesson Focus
Head lice are insects that can spread from one person to another.

Vocabulary
head lice

Head lice are tiny insects. They can live on a person's head. The lice lay sticky eggs on hair. The lice bite the skin on the head and make it itch.

Special shampoos kill head lice and their eggs. Then the eggs must be pulled off or combed out. After a few days the itching stops.

Head lice are very tiny. They are smaller than grains of rice.

Head lice can spread from person to person. Following these rules will help keep you from getting head lice from others.

► Do not put heads together when talking or playing with a friend.

► Do not share brushes, combs, hats, headphones, or helmets.

► Do not share clothes or pillows with a person who has head lice.

Why shouldn't you share these objects?

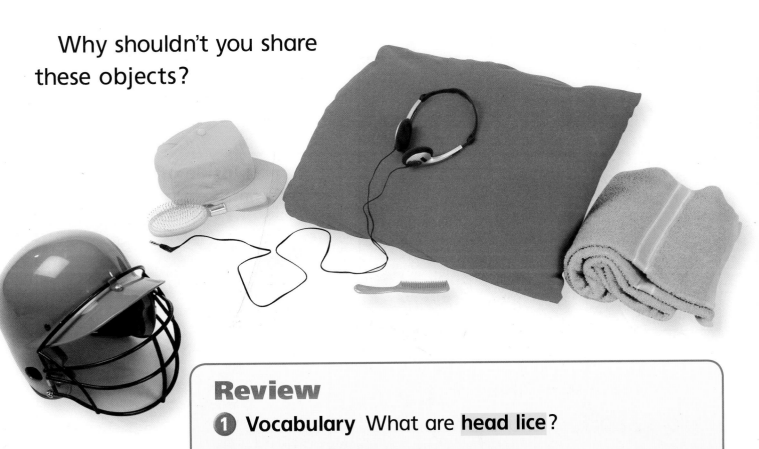

Review

1 **Vocabulary** What are **head lice**?

2 How do you get rid of head lice?

3 Make a poster that shows ways to keep from getting head lice.

Caring for Eyes and Ears

You use your eyes in many ways. Your eyes see the colors, shapes, and sizes of everything around you. Your sense of sight lets you read books and see signs.

Outside of Eye

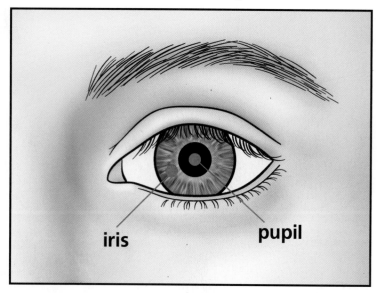

iris

pupil

Inside of Eye

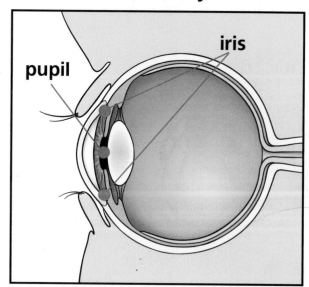

pupil

iris

An eye has a white part, a colored part, and a black part. The colored part is the iris. The black part is the pupil.

Caring for Your Eyes

▶ Have a doctor check your eyes to find out if they are healthy.

▶ Keep sharp objects away from your eyes.

▶ Don't rub your eyes with dirty hands.

▶ Wear sunglasses if you are in the sun.

▶ Wear goggles when you play sports that can hurt your eyes.

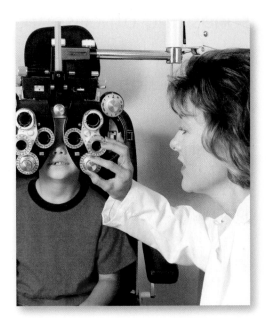

Your sense of hearing lets you enjoy songs and other sounds. Your ears hear voices, car horns, and fire alarms, and they let you listen to directions.

What you see on the outside of your head is only part of your ear. The main part of your ear is inside your head.

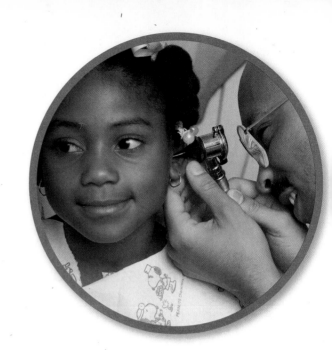

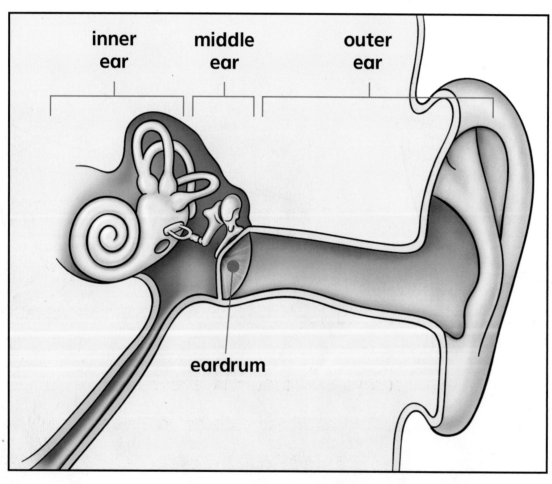

inner ear   middle ear   outer ear

eardrum

Inside of Ear   **Outside of Ear**

Caring for Your Ears

► Have a doctor test your hearing. Finding a problem early makes it easier to fix.

► Protect your ears when you play sports.

► Keep your ears clean.

► Never put anything in your ears.

► Keep your ears warm in winter.

► Protect your ears from loud noises.

Review

1 How can you protect your eyes?

2 Why should you take care of your ears?

3 Write a list of ways to take care of your eyes and ears.

Communicate

When you are ill or hurt, you may need help. **Communicate**, or tell, your problem to a parent or another trusted adult.

1 Figure out what the problem is. Then decide who can help you.

Kathy feels pain in her ear. She is not sure what to do. She looks for her dad to get help.

2 Say what you need to say. Use body language if necessary.

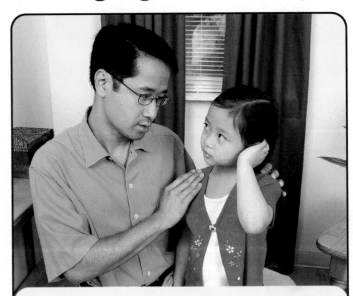

Kathy tells her dad that her ear hurts. She also shows him where the pain is.

3 Listen carefully.
Answer any questions.

Kathy's dad asks if she feels hot or has other pains. She answers his questions clearly.

4 Get information.

Kathy's dad wants to find ways to help Kathy feel better. He calls the family doctor for help.

 Problem Solving

Use the steps to solve this problem.

You are in class. Your head hurts. Then your stomach starts to hurt. How should you communicate your problem?

Product Labels and Ads

You and your parents use many products that help keep you healthy. You should know about a product before you buy it. To find out about a product, read its label.

A **label** lists what is in a product. It tells what the product does. Compare product labels and prices. This helps you choose the best product for you.

Steps for Choosing a Product

1 Decide if the product is something you need or something you want.

2 Compare several brands.

3 Choose the product that will meet your needs the best.

4 Use the product. Does it meet your needs? Would you buy it again?

Compare these labels. Which soap would you buy? Why?

Bar Soap
Natural
Fragrance Free
NET WT 4.5 OZ (127g)

Hand Soap
FRESH FLOWER SCENT
GENTLE ON SKIN
11.25 FL OZ (332 mL)

An **ad** tries to get you to buy something. Some ads give you good information. Others try to trick you.

How to Think About Ads

1 Figure out why the ad was made.

2 Watch for tricks that try to make you agree with the ad. Ads may use bright colors or loud music. Ads may use a famous person.

3 Find out if the information in the ad is true.

4 Find out if any information is left out of the ad.

What should you watch out for in the ads in the picture?

Review

1 **Vocabulary** What is an **ad**?

2 What can you learn from a product's label?

3 Make your own ad for sunglasses. Draw and write about the sunglasses.

ACTIVITIES

Math

How many hours did children play outside on Tuesday?

How many hours did they play on Thursday?

On what days did they play for the same number of hours?

Make your own graph about playing outside.

Hours Playing Outside				
Monday	☀	☀	☀	
Tuesday	☀	☀	☀	☀
Wednesday	☀			
Thursday	☀	☀		
Friday	☀	☀	☀	

Writing

Compare Two Products

Compare two kinds of soap, shampoo, or toothpaste. How are they the same? How are they different? Make a chart and fill it in. Then use the information in your chart to write about the products.

SHAMPOOS	
Same	Different
in bottles	one is white and one is pink

GO ONLINE For more activities, visit The Learning Site.
www.harcourtschool.com/health

Respect

Building Good Character

Developing Self-Respect

When you show **respect** for others, you show them you are caring and thoughtful. You can also show self-respect, or respect for yourself. When you keep clean and help yourself stay healthy, you show respect for yourself. You feel and look good.

How is this boy showing self-respect?

Activity

Act out a way to show self-respect. Ask your classmates to guess what you are acting out.

Use Health Words

Tell which picture goes with the word or words.

a.

b.

1. head lice
2. sunscreen
3. germs
4. sunburn
5. respect

c.

d.

e.

 Reading Skill

6. You are going to a picnic. Make a prediction about using sunscreen. Write about what you think will happen.

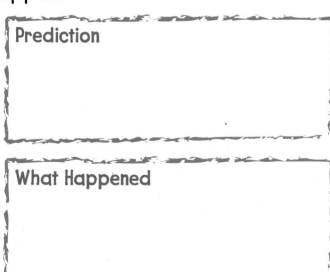

Prediction

What Happened

Use Life Skills

Look at the picture. Then answer the questions.

7 What is Kathy doing about the pain in her ear?

8 What are four steps that can help you communicate about a health need?

Write About It

9 Make up an ad about a health-care product you use. Draw a picture of it. How does the product keep you healthy? Write about why others should buy it.

Super Shine Shampoo makes your hair super shiny!

3 Caring for Your Teeth

Reading Skill

Use Context Clues

The words, pictures, and charts near a new word can help you read and understand it.

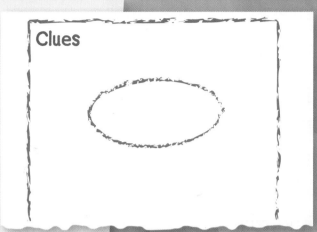

Clues

Health Graph

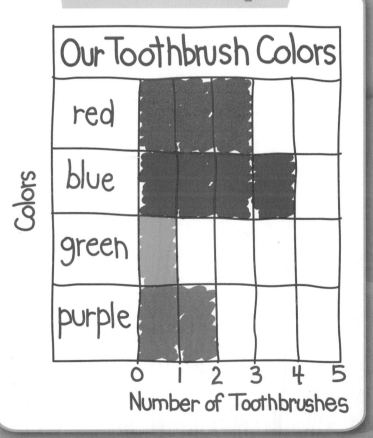

Our Toothbrush Colors

Colors

red
blue
green
purple

0 1 2 3 4 5
Number of Toothbrushes

Daily Physical Activity

Brush and floss your teeth every day. You should also exercise every day.

 **Be Active!**

Use **Late for Supper** on Track 3.

Healthy Teeth and Gums

Lesson Focus
Eating the right foods helps keep your teeth healthy.

Vocabulary
primary teeth
permanent teeth
cavity

Your teeth are very important. You use them to bite and chew food.

When you look at your teeth in a mirror, you can see only part of each tooth. The other part is hidden under your gums.

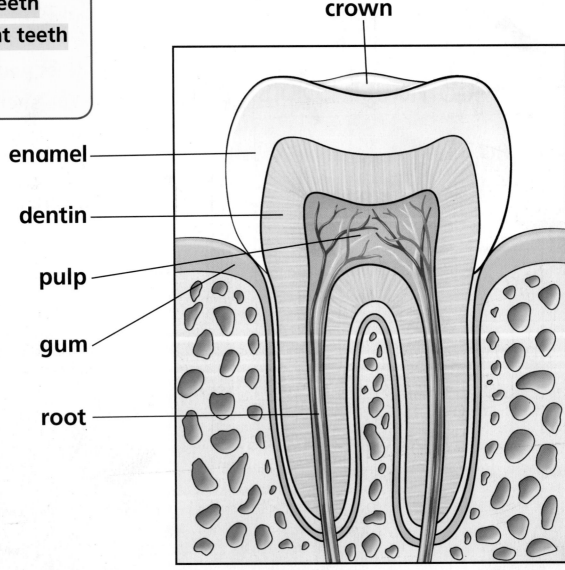

crown

enamel

dentin

pulp

gum

root

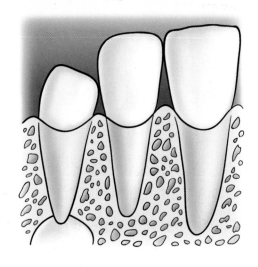

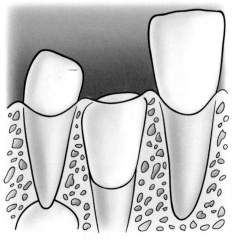

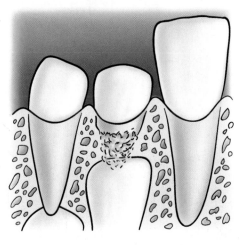

You get two sets of teeth as you grow. The first teeth are **primary teeth**. They start to grow in when you are about six months old. Children have about twenty primary teeth.

You begin to lose your primary teeth when you are about six years old. A new set of teeth takes their place. These teeth are **permanent teeth**. Adults can have thirty-two permanent teeth.

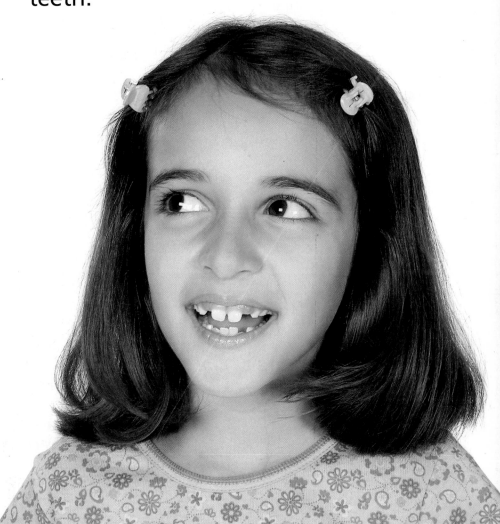

Eating the right foods helps keep your teeth and gums healthy. Foods like milk, yogurt, and cheese help your teeth stay strong. Fruits and vegetables help them, too.

Sugar is not good for your teeth. If sugar stays on your teeth too long, you can get a cavity. A **cavity** is a hole in a tooth. Eat sweets only with meals. Then brush your teeth. For snacks, eat fresh fruits and vegetables.

How do the foods on the tray help keep your teeth healthy?

Review

1. **Vocabulary** What is a **cavity**?

2. What happens to your primary teeth?

3. Draw and label pictures of two foods that are good for your teeth.

Caring for Your Teeth and Gums

Lesson Focus
Brushing and flossing your teeth keeps them clean and healthy.

Vocabulary
floss

Brushing your teeth and gums keeps them clean and healthy. Brushing gets the sugar and food off your teeth.

You should brush your teeth at least twice a day. Brush in the morning. Brush again before you go to bed at night. If you can, brush after you eat, too. Always use your own toothbrush.

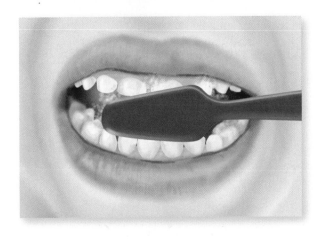

First, brush the outsides of your teeth. Do not scrub hard. Move the brush gently.

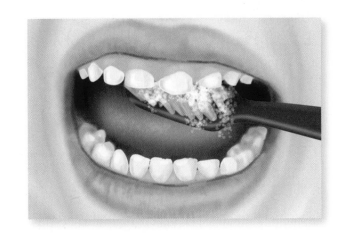

Next, brush the insides of your teeth.

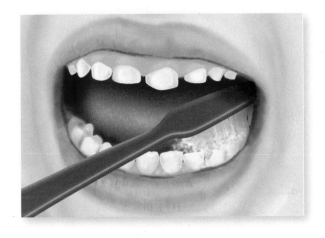

Then, brush the flat parts of your back teeth, which chew food.

Brush your tongue. Last, rinse your mouth with water. Do not swallow the toothpaste.

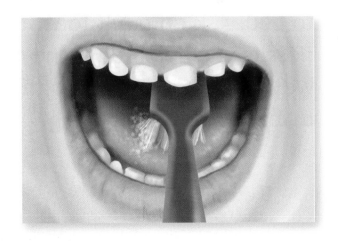

Labels on toothpaste tubes tell you to use only a small amount of toothpaste. It should be about the size of a pea.

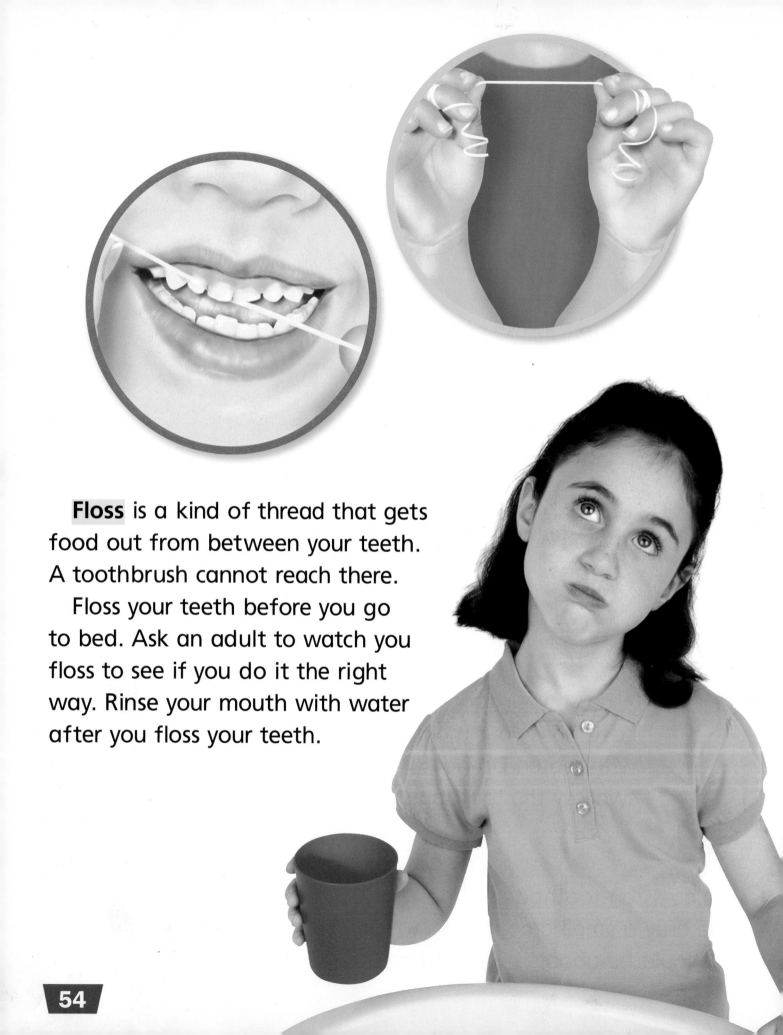

Floss is a kind of thread that gets food out from between your teeth. A toothbrush cannot reach there.

Floss your teeth before you go to bed. Ask an adult to watch you floss to see if you do it the right way. Rinse your mouth with water after you floss your teeth.

There are many products for cleaning teeth. Some products cost more than others. The products look and taste different. They also have different things in them. To learn what is in the products, read their labels.

What do the labels tell you about these products?

Review

1 **Vocabulary** Why should you **floss** your teeth?

2 When should you brush your teeth?

3 Make a toothpaste label. On it, write about how to use the toothpaste and why it will help your teeth.

Set Goals

Caring for your teeth will keep them healthy. You can set a **goal** you want to work toward. How can you set a goal to take good care of your teeth?

1 **Set a goal.**

Mike sometimes forgets to floss his teeth. He talks to his mom. Then he sets a goal. His goal is to floss his teeth each night.

2 **Make a plan to meet the goal.**

Mike wants to make sure he flosses his teeth every night. He makes a calendar. He will mark it each night that he flosses.

56

❸ Work toward the goal.

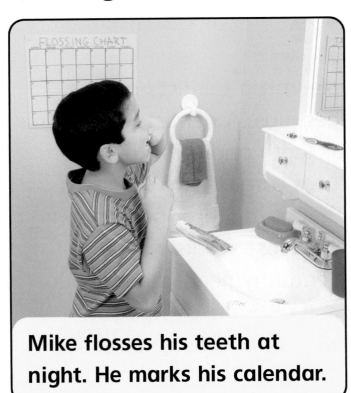

Mike flosses his teeth at night. He marks his calendar.

❹ Ask yourself how you are doing.

Mike looks at his calendar after one week. He flossed his teeth every night except one. Mike will keep working toward his goal.

💡 Problem Solving

Use the steps to solve this problem.

You want to eat foods that help your teeth stay strong. What can you do to meet this goal? How can you keep track of what you do and how you are doing?

The Dentist's Office

Lesson Focus
Dentists and dental hygienists help you keep your teeth healthy.

Vocabulary
dental hygienist

Many people visit a dentist's office for regular checkups. A dentist helps you keep your teeth and gums healthy. The dentist takes care of any problems you have with your teeth or gums.

A **dental hygienist** works with a dentist. The dental hygienist cleans your teeth. He or she also makes sure you know how to brush and floss correctly.

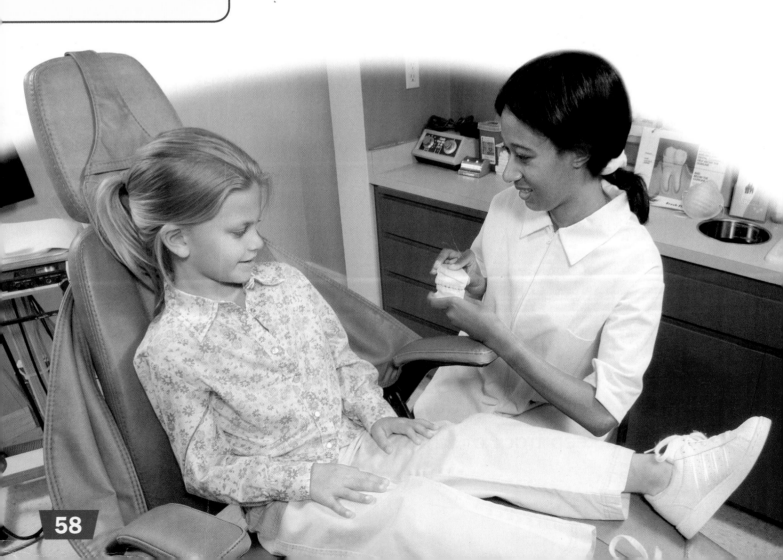

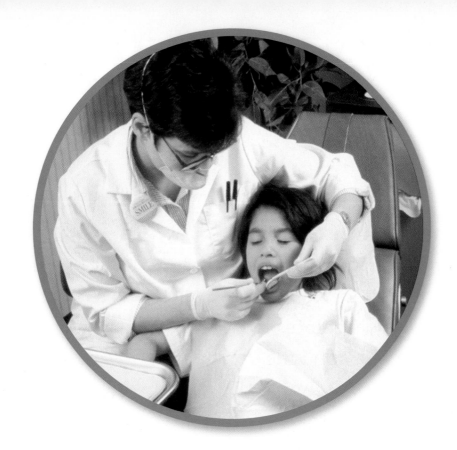

If you do not brush and floss often enough, you may get a cavity. A dentist can fix a cavity.

The dentist uses a drill to clean out the hole in the tooth. Then he or she fills the hole with a hard material.

If the dentist finds a cavity or other problem early, it is easier to fix.

Review

1 **Vocabulary** What is a **dental hygienist**?

2 How does a dentist fix a cavity?

3 Write a list of reasons it is important to visit a dentist for regular checkups.

Math

Permanent Teeth Graph

Who has the most permanent teeth?

What is the difference between the most and the fewest?

Make your own graph about teeth.

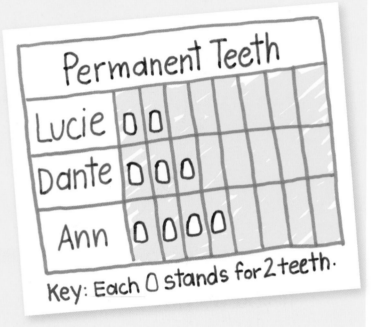

Permanent Teeth

Lucie	0	0					
Dante	0	0	0				
Ann	0	0	0	0			

Key: Each 0 stands for 2 teeth.

Writing

Information on a Label

Look at a toothpaste tube. What information can you find on the label? Make a list of all the kinds of information on the label.

What I Read on a Tube of Toothpaste

1. how to use toothpaste
2. what is in toothpaste
3. warnings

GO ONLINE For more activities, visit The Learning Site.
www.harcourtschool.com/health

Honesty

Being Honest About Taking Care of Your Teeth

When you are **honest**, people know you are truthful and can be trusted. Your parents or dentist may ask you how well you are brushing and flossing your teeth. You tell them the truth. You tell your parents if one of your teeth hurts. When you do this, they can help you feel better.

How is this girl showing she is honest?

Activity

Work with a partner. Tell why it is important to be honest with your parents and your dentist.

61

Chapter Review

Use Health Words

Use the words to tell about the pictures.

1 permanent teeth

2 cavity

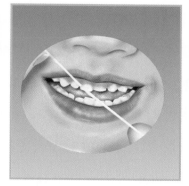

3 floss

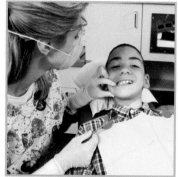

4 dental hygienist

Reading Skill

5 Use the clues in the box to figure out the words that belong in the center.

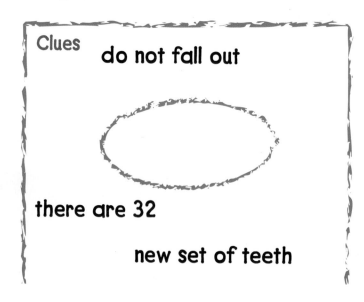

Clues

do not fall out

there are 32

new set of teeth

Use Life Skills

Look at the pictures. Then answer the questions.

a.

b.

6 Which picture shows Mike making a plan to meet his goal?

7 What are four steps that can help you set and reach goals?

Write About It

8 Write some ways you can take care of your teeth. Write some ways a dentist and a dental hygienist can help you.

I floss my teeth each night.

Food for Fitness

Find Cause and Effect

An effect is something that happens. A cause is the reason something happens.

Cause		Effect
	→	

Health Graph

What We Like in Salads

tomatoes	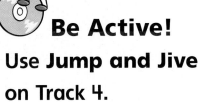
lettuce	☺ ☺
onions	☺
peppers	☺ ☺ ☺

Key: Each ☺ stands for 10 children.

Daily Physical Activity

Eat foods that are good for you every day. Exercise every day, too.

Be Active!
Use **Jump and Jive** on Track 4.

Your Body Uses Food

Lesson Focus
Your body uses food in many ways.

Vocabulary
energy

Your body uses the food you eat to make the energy you need. **Energy** is the power that lets you do things. You need energy to move, speak, play, study, and do all the other things you do each day.

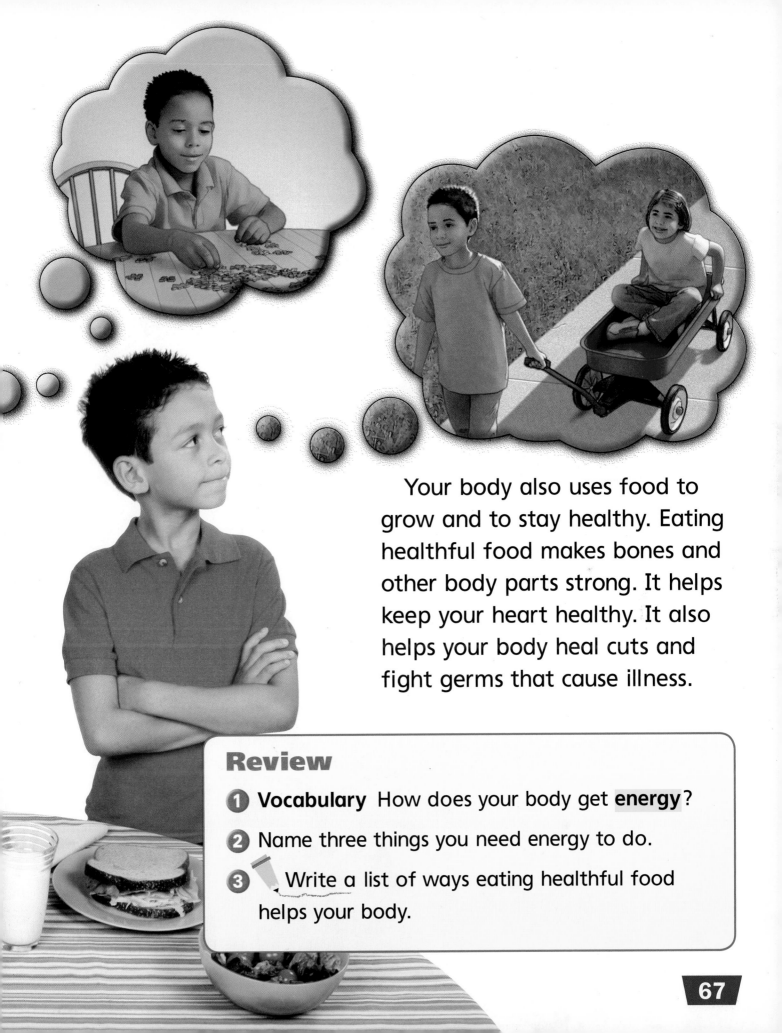

Your body also uses food to grow and to stay healthy. Eating healthful food makes bones and other body parts strong. It helps keep your heart healthy. It also helps your body heal cuts and fight germs that cause illness.

Review

1. **Vocabulary** How does your body get **energy**?

2. Name three things you need energy to do.

3. Write a list of ways eating healthful food helps your body.

Knowing What to Eat and Drink

Lesson Focus
Choose foods and drinks that are healthful.

Vocabulary
MyPyramid
wastes

Grains

Vegetables

Your body needs different kinds of foods. **MyPyramid** helps you choose what you will eat. It shows which group each food belongs to and how much of it to eat. Eat more foods from the wider stripes of the pyramid. Eat fewer foods from the more narrow stripes.

Fruits

Milk

Meat and Beans

Your adult family members can help you choose foods that are good for you. They can also make sure that you eat many kinds of foods. This will help you stay healthy. Different foods make different parts of your body strong.

Name the different foods at this picnic. Which food groups do they belong to?

You need water to stay healthy. It helps get rid of wastes. **Wastes** are things your body does not need. You also need water to make sweat. Sweat cools your body when it is hot.

Drink six to eight cups of water each day. Eating vegetables and fruits also gives your body water.

Review

Vocabulary How can **MyPyramid** help you stay healthy?

Name two ways your adult family members can help you eat healthful foods.

Write a healthful menu for breakfast.

Eating Healthful Meals

Lesson Focus
Choose healthful foods for your meals.

Vocabulary
meal
fat
balanced diet
ingredients

A **meal** is the food you eat at a certain time each day. Breakfast, lunch, and dinner are meals. Many people eat these three meals each day. Healthful meals give your body the energy it needs.

breakfast

lunch

dinner

Some foods are more healthful than others. Choose foods that do not have a lot of fat, sugar, or salt.

Fat is a part of food that gives your body energy. You need some fat, but eating too much fat is not healthful.

Some foods have a lot of fat. People who eat too many of these foods can gain too much weight. They can also get heart disease.

There are many foods to choose from. Choose foods that give you a balanced diet. A **balanced diet** has the right amount of foods from each food group. A balanced diet gives your body everything it needs to stay healthy. If you have a balanced diet, you will feel well, strong, and full of energy.

Dietary Fiber   25g   30g

Calories per gram:
Fat 9 • Carbohydrate 4 • Protein 4

INGREDIENTS: WHOLE GRAIN OAT FLOUR (INCLUDES THE OAT BRAN), MARSHMALLOWS (SUGAR, CORN SYRUP, DEXTROSE, MODIFIED FOOD STARCH, GELATIN, ARTIFICIAL AND NATURAL FLAVOR, YELLOW 5 & 6, RED 40, BLUE 1, BLUE 2), SUGAR, WHEAT STARCH, CORN SYRUP, SALT, CALCIUM CARBONATE, COLOR ADDED, DICALCIUM PHOS-PHATE, TRISODIUM PHOSPHATE, ARTIFICIAL FLAVOR, VITAMIN C (SODIUM ASCORBATE), ZINC AND IRON (MIN-ERAL NUTRIENTS), A B VITAMIN (NIACINAMIDE), BHT (A PRESERVATIVE), VITAMIN B_6 (PYRIDOXINE HYDRO-CHLORIDE), VITAMIN B_2 (RIBOFLAVIN), VITAMIN B_1 (THIAMIN MONONITRATE), VITAMIN A PALMITATE, A B VITAMIN (FOLIC ACID), VITAMIN B_{12}, VITAMIN D.

Cholest	Less than	300mg	300mg
Sodium	Less than	2,400mg	2,400mg
Potassium		3,500mg	3,500mg
Total Carb		300g	375g
Fiber		25g	30g

INGREDIENTS: WHOLE GRAIN WHEAT FLOUR, WHEAT FLOUR, MALTED BARLEY FLOUR, SALT, DRIED YEAST.
VITAMINS AND MINERALS: REDUCED IRON, NIACIN, VITAMIN B6, ZINC OXIDE (SOURCE OF ZINC), VITAMIN A PALMITATE, THIAMIN MONONITRATE (VITAMIN B1), RIBOFLAVIN (VITAMIN B2), FOLIC ACID, VITAMIN B12, VITAMIN D.

Read food labels to choose healthful foods. Look at the ingredients. The **ingredients** are the things the food is made from. They are listed in order from most to least. Choose foods that do not have a lot of fat, sugar, or salt.

Compare the ingredients in these two cereals. Which cereal is more healthful? Why?

Review

1. **Vocabulary** What are the three **meals** that many people eat each day?

2. What can happen if you eat a lot of fat?

3. Write a shopping list for dinner. Choose foods that make a balanced diet.

Ads Affect Food Choices

Lesson Focus

Do not let ads trick you into buying foods that are not healthful.

Ads for fast foods, breakfast cereals, and other foods try to get you to buy what a company makes. Ads may offer a free toy. Some ads use a famous person, funny jokes, or exciting music.

Ads tell you the food tastes good. They don't tell you if it has a lot of fat, sugar, or salt. They don't tell you if other foods are more healthful.

When you see an ad for a food, look for tricks. Think about whether the information about the food is true. Find out whether the food is healthful.

When you choose a breakfast cereal, do not think about which one has the more exciting ads. Choose the cereal that is more healthful.

You may have seen ads for fast foods. Some fast foods have a lot of fat, sugar, or salt. Other fast-food choices are better for your health. If you eat fast food, you can make healthful choices.

Many things may keep you from making good food choices. A friend may offer you a candy bar. Stores and restaurants sell foods that have too much fat, sugar, or salt. Ads try to make you want unhealthful foods.

Your adult family members can help you choose good foods. You and your family are responsible for making healthful food choices.

Review

1. Name two ways an ad may try to make you want to buy a food.

2. What can you do to make a good decision when you eat fast food?

3. Write an ad that tries to trick people into buying a snack food.

Make Decisions

Some snacks have a lot of sugar and fat. Some snacks have a lot of salt. Other snacks are more healthful. When you want a snack, make good **decisions**, or choices. These steps show how.

1 **Think about the choices.**

Rita can buy a snack that has fat and sugar, a salty snack, or a more healthful snack.

2 **Say NO to choices that are against your family rules.**

Rita says NO to the candy. She knows her parents do not want her to eat snacks that have sugar and fat.

3 Ask yourself what could happen with each choice.

4 Make the best choice.

The popcorn might make Rita thirsty. She wants something juicy.

Rita decides to buy an apple. It tastes good!

 Problem Solving

Use the steps to solve this problem.

At a party, some of your friends are snacking on potato chips and cookies. Others are eating grapes. Which snack will you choose? How can you make your decision?

Handling Foods Safely

Wash fresh fruits and vegetables before you eat them. This gets rid of germs. Cooking food also gets rid of germs.

Wash your hands with soap before you touch any food. Also wash them after you touch uncooked meat or eggs. Be sure your cup, plate, bowl, glass, fork, and spoon are washed, too.

All foods should be covered and put away. Germs can get on uncovered foods. Storing foods safely keeps germs from getting on them.

Meat, milk, and some other foods must stay cold. Keep them in the refrigerator. They can spoil, or become bad, if they are not cold. Spoiled food may have germs that can make you ill.

Review

1 Why is it important to wash your hands before and after handling foods?

2 How can you store foods safely?

3 Write a list of rules for making sure that foods are safe to eat.

ACTIVITIES

Math

Sandwiches Graph

How many children chose turkey sandwiches?

Which sandwich did the most children choose?

Make your own graph about choosing healthful sandwiches.

Sandwiches We Like

tuna	☺	☺		
cheese	☺			
peanut butter	☺	☺	☺	☺
turkey	☺	☺	☺	

Key: Each ☺ stands for 10 children.

Writing

Make a Healthful Meal

Write a menu for a healthful family meal. Choose foods from the groups on MyPyramid. Prepare your meal with your family. Make sure you handle the food safely.

Family Dinner Menu

grilled chicken

rice

peas and carrots

fruit salad

low-fat milk

 For more activities, visit The Learning Site.
www.harcourtschool.com/health

Honesty

Being Honest About Foods

Adults in your family may say not to eat foods with a lot of salt, sugar, or fat. They may say not to eat snacks before meals.

A friend may offer you a snack that your parents do not want you to eat. Follow what your parents tell you even when they are not around. Show **honesty** by telling the truth about what you eat. If you are honest, people know they can trust you.

How is this girl honest with her parents?

Activity

List ways to be honest about food choices.

85

Chapter Review

Use Health Words

Use the words to tell about the pictures.

1 energy

2 meal

3 ingredients

4 MyPyramid

Reading Skill

5 Tell some causes for this effect.

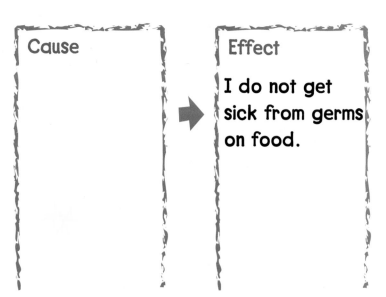

Cause	Effect
	I do not get sick from germs on food.

Use Life Skills

Look at the pictures. Then answer the questions.

6 Which picture shows the more healthful snack?

7 Name four steps you can use to make good decisions about snacks.

Write About It

8 Draw a picture of a healthful meal. Write about why it is healthful.

This cereal is healthful. It does not have a lot of sugar.

Keeping Fit and Active

Find the Main Idea

The main idea of something you are reading is what it is mostly about. The details tell more about it.

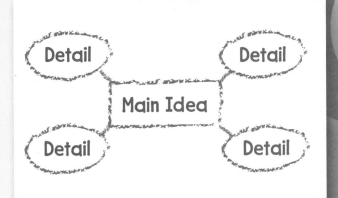

Health Graph

Activities We Like

soccer
T-ball
swimming
running

Activities

0 10 20 30 40 50
Number of Children

Daily Physical Activity

Exercise, eat healthful foods, and rest to help you stay fit.

 **Be Active!**

Use **Flexercise** on Track 5.

Physical Fitness

Using your body in an active way is called **exercise**. Exercise makes you fit. When you are **fit**, your body is able to be active or play hard for a long time without getting tired.

How are these people staying fit?

Exercise keeps your body healthy. It helps make your heart and your other muscles strong. It helps your lungs work better, too.

Exercise is also good for your brain. Exercise helps your brain get more oxygen. This helps you think and learn new things.

Exercise makes you look good and feel good. It gives you energy to do things. Exercise can also make you feel better when you are upset. It helps you stop thinking about what made you upset. Exercise can help keep you healthy and happy.

Best of all, exercise is fun. You can exercise at home or at school. You can exercise with your family and your friends. Playing games and sports is a good way to exercise and be active.

Review

1 **Vocabulary** What does being **fit** mean?

2 How is exercise good for your body?

3 Write about three ways you can exercise at home.

93

Manage Stress

When you feel worried or excited, you feel **stress**. Stress can make your head or your stomach hurt. Stress can make it hard to eat or sleep. How can you manage stress?

1 **Know what stress feels like.**

Paul's father will bring home a new kitten in an hour. Paul is excited. His muscles feel tight. His heart beats quickly.

2 **Figure out why you feel stress.**

Paul feels stress because he must wait. Waiting is hard because he really wants to see the kitten.

3 Do something active to help yourself feel better.

Paul finds a way to stop thinking about his stress for a while. He plays in his yard.

4 Talk with someone about the stress.

Paul plays catch with his sister. Talking and playing with her helps him manage his stress.

 Problem Solving

Use the steps to solve this problem.

You will be getting a haircut in about an hour. You are worried about whether you will look good with your new haircut. How could you manage your stress?

Exercising Safely

Safety is always important when you exercise. **Safety** is staying away from danger or harm. Exercising safely helps keep you from getting hurt. Follow these four steps each time you exercise.

2 Stretch your muscles.

1 Warm up your body before you exercise.

3 Start out slowly. Then you can go faster.

4 After you exercise, cool down. Stretch your muscles again.

Rules tell you what to do. Follow the safety rules on the sign when you play or exercise. Following the rules will help keep you from getting hurt.

Rules for Exercising Safely

Drink a lot of water when you exercise.

Rest when you are tired.

Stop if you feel pain.

Do not exercise outside if it is very hot.

Wear the right clothes and safety gear.

Wear safety gear when you exercise. It will help keep you from getting hurt. A helmet protects your head. A mouth guard keeps your teeth safe. Goggles protect your eyes. Safety pads protect your knees and elbows. Wrist guards protect your wrists. Shoes that fit right protect your feet.

How are these girls exercising safely?

Review

1 **Vocabulary** Why is **safety** important?

2 Make a poster to show how to protect your body when you exercise.

3 Write three safety rules to follow when you exercise.

99

Getting Enough Sleep

Lesson Focus
Your body needs sleep to stay healthy.

Your body needs to rest each day. Your body rests and fixes itself as you sleep. Getting enough sleep helps you stay healthy.

Sometimes stress makes it hard to fall asleep. Reading or finding other ways to relax may help you go to sleep. Going to bed at the same time each night helps, too.

You feel better when you have had enough sleep. You have more energy to do things. If you don't get enough sleep, you may feel tired or grouchy.

Sleep is also good for your brain. It is easier to learn when you have had enough sleep.

Review

1. What can make it hard to fall asleep?

2. How can you tell if you are getting enough sleep?

3. Write about things you can do to relax before you go to sleep.

ACTIVITIES

 ## Math

Kickball Graph

How many minutes did Mya's class play kickball?

Which class played for the most minutes?

How many minutes in all did the classes play?

Make your own graph about playing sports.

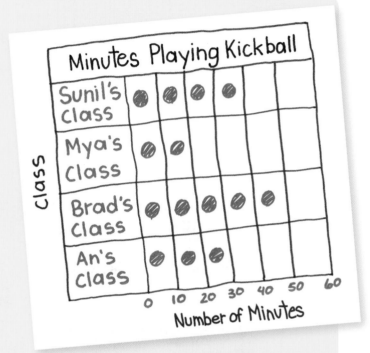

 ## Writing

Exercise Plan

Think of the physical activities you like best. On what days of the week will you do them? How long will you do each one? Write your plan in a chart.

My Exercise Plan

Sunday	Ride bike 20 min. Play basketball 30 min.
Monday	
Tuesday	
Wednesday	
Thursday	
Friday	
Saturday	

 For more activities, visit The Learning Site.
www.harcourtschool.com/health

Fairness

Listening to Others

You know you should show fairness to other people. **Fairness** means treating everyone in the same way.

One way to be fair is to listen to others. Think about what they have to say. Let them finish talking. Then you can have your turn to talk. Listening to others shows respect. When you respect others, they will respect you.

How are these girls showing fairness?

Activity

Work with a partner. Talk about ways to be fair. Take turns talking and listening.

Chapter Review

Use Health Words

Use the word to tell about the picture.

1 fit

2 exercise

3 rules

4 safety

(Focus Skill) Reading Skill

5 Tell the main idea.

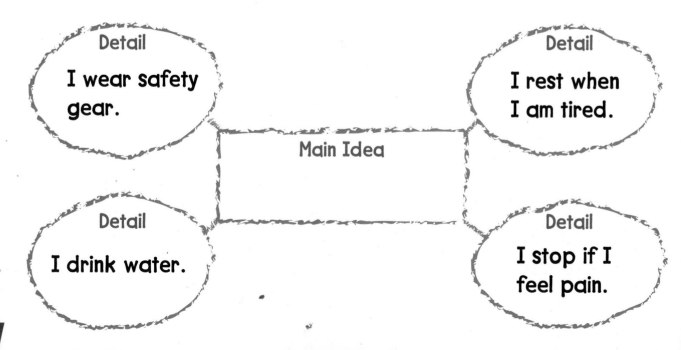

Detail

I wear safety gear.

Detail

I rest when I am tired.

Main Idea

Detail

I drink water.

Detail

I stop if I feel pain.

Use Life Skills

Look at the picture. Then answer the questions.

6 How can you tell that Paul is not feeling stress now?

7 What are four steps you can use to manage stress?

Write About It

8 Write about the four steps you should follow when you exercise.

Start out slowly.

Avoiding Danger

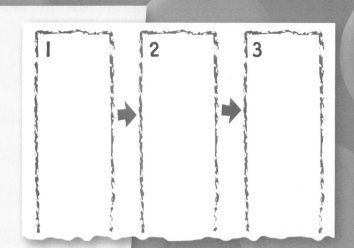

Sequence

When you sequence things, you put them in the order in which they happen.

Health Graph

Safe Places to Play	
park	🧍🧍🧍🧍
backyard	🧍
friend's house	🧍🧍🧍🧍🧍🧍
playground	🧍🧍🧍

Key: Each 🧍 stands for 5 children.

Daily Physical Activity

You should exercise every day. Follow the rules for safe exercise.

 Be Active!

Use **Muscle Mambo** on Track 6.

Staying Safe from Fires

You can help prevent fires from starting. Follow these rules.

► Never play with matches or lighters.

► Do not touch lit candles.

► Do not cook unless an adult is with you.

► Be careful around stoves, fireplaces, and grills.

► Do not touch electric cords, plugs, or outlets.

If your clothes catch fire, do these things right away. Stop! Drop! Roll! Get help from an adult once the fire is out. If someone else is on fire, yell STOP! DROP! ROLL! Practice doing Stop, Drop, and Roll. It will help you be ready if this happens to you.

1 Stop. Walking or running makes the fire worse.

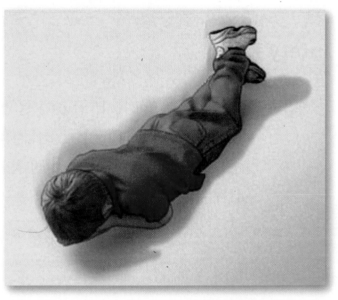

2 Drop. Lie down quickly on the ground. Cover your face and eyes.

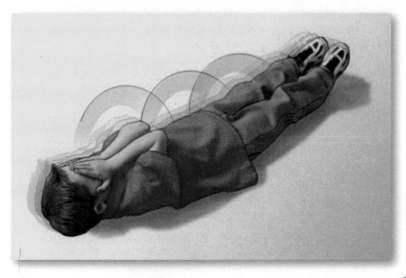

3 Roll. Roll over and over until the flames go out.

Fire drills are part of good fire safety. **Fire drills** let you practice getting out of a building safely if it is on fire. Schools have drills for fires. They may have earthquake drills, tornado drills, or other drills, too. You should have drills at home. Having drills helps prepare you and your family for emergencies.

Fire Safety Rules

► Make sure your home has smoke alarms that work.

► Practice fire drills with your family.

► Choose a place outside your home to meet if there is a fire.

► Know two ways to leave each room. If a closed door feels hot, do not open it. Use another way out.

► Do not hide under a bed or in a closet during a fire.

► Get out quickly if there is a fire in your home. Drop to the floor and crawl if the room is filled with smoke.

► Use Stop, Drop, and Roll if your clothes catch fire.

► Call 911 from outside your home.

► Never go back into a burning building.

The phone number to call in an emergency is **911**. Call 911 if there is a fire. Tell the 911 operator your name, address, and phone number. Follow the operator's instructions.

Review

1. **Vocabulary** When should you call **911**?

2. Tell what to do if your clothes catch fire.

3. Write a list of fire safety rules. Ask your family to help you.

Staying Safe from Weapons

Lesson Focus
Stay away from weapons so you do not get hurt.

Vocabulary
weapons

Weapons are guns, knives, and other things that can hurt you. Never touch any weapon if a parent or other trusted adult is not around. You can hurt or even kill yourself or someone else if you play with a weapon. Never point a weapon at yourself or at anyone else.

Hand Gun

Knife

ng Shot

If you find a weapon, do not touch it. Leave the place right away. Tell an adult you can trust. The adult can be a parent, a teacher, a police officer, or a crossing guard.

If a friend wants to show you a weapon, say NO and leave. Tell an adult family member as soon as you get home.

Review

1. **Vocabulary** What are **weapons**?

2. What should you do if you find a gun?

3. Write about what you should do if a friend wants you to play with a weapon.

Staying Safe from Poisons

Lesson Focus
Stay away from poisons so you do not become ill.

Vocabulary
poisons

Poisons are things that make you ill if they get into your body. Some poisons can even kill you. Never eat, taste, touch, or smell poisons.

Many poisons are used in the home. Paint and bug spray can be poisons. Cleaning products can be poisons, too. Even medicines can be poisons if they are not used correctly.

Do not go near any poisons. Only adults can use them safely. You and a trusted adult can find out if something is a poison by reading its label.

DANGER!

If a poison gets into your body, tell an adult right away. If an adult is not around, call 911. The 911 operator will send help.

Review

1. **Vocabulary** Why should you stay away from **poisons**?

2. What should you do if a poison gets into your body?

3. Write a list of rules for staying safe from poisons. Make a poster that shows your rules.

Staying Safe Around Strangers

Strangers are people you do not know well. Some strangers are dangerous. To be safe, do not talk to strangers. Never walk anywhere with them or get into a car with them.

If a stranger walks up to you and bothers you, yell NO! and run away. Tell a parent or an adult you can trust.

If a stranger calls to you from a car, do not stop and talk. Yell NO! and run away.

Do not give your name, phone number, or address to a stranger. If you are lost, get help from an adult you can trust. Find a police officer, a guard, or a store clerk.

If a stranger knocks on your door, do not answer. Do not tell someone on the phone that you are alone.

Use the Internet only with a parent, a teacher, or another adult you trust. It is not safe to write to strangers.

Review

1. **Vocabulary** Why should you stay away from **strangers**?

2. What should you do if a stranger asks you to help him or her look for something?

3. Write about some adults you can trust. Tell how they can help you.

Refuse

You can play safely by refusing to do unsafe things. To **refuse** is to say NO. Here are some steps you can use to say NO.

1 **Say NO and tell why not.**

Come on, let's play!

No. My parents don't let me play in the street.

Joanna asks Brad to play a game in the street. Brad refuses. His parents have told him that playing in the street is not safe.

2 **Think about what could happen.**

Brad tells Joanna a car might hit them in the street. Or a stranger in a car might bother them.

3 Suggest something else to do.

Brad says they could play in his yard instead. Joanna doesn't want to. She says her toy once got stuck in a tree in Brad's yard.

4 Laugh about it!

Brad says they should go to the playground. He says it does not have trees that eat toys! The children laugh and go to the playground.

Problem Solving

Use the steps to solve this problem.

A friend asks you to go skating with her. Neither of you has a helmet or other safety gear. How can you refuse to go with her?

ACTIVITIES

Math

Swimming Graph

How many minutes can Mehar swim?

How many minutes can Sal swim?

Who can swim for the most minutes?

Make your own graph about swimming.

Minutes We Can Swim			
Dara	◔	◔	◔
Mehar	◔	◔	
Minh	◔	◔	
Sal	◔		

Key: Each ◔ stands for 5 minutes.

Writing

Safety Rules

What should you do if you are lost? Make a list of rules to follow. Write about how following each rule will help you stay safe.

What to Do If You Are Lost

1. Find a police officer or another grown-up you can trust.

2.

3.

 For more activities, visit The Learning Site.
www.harcourtschool.com/health

Responsibility

Getting Attention in Responsible Ways

Be responsible when you want to get attention. When you are **responsible**, you think about others as well as yourself.

Be polite. Do not yell or say things that could bother others. Be safe. Do not do things that could hurt you or others.

How are these children getting attention in a responsible way?

Activity

Work with a partner. Act out responsible ways to get attention.

121

Use Health Words

Use the word to tell about the picture.

1 911

2 weapons

3 poison

4 stranger

Reading Skill

5 Sequence these words–Drop, Stop, Roll.
Write a sentence for each word.

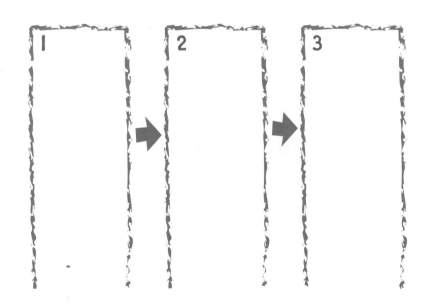

Use Life Skills

Look at the picture. Then answer the questions.

6 How can Brad refuse to play in the street?

7 How can you refuse to do something that is not safe?

Write About It

8 Write a list of things your family can do to stay safe from fires.

We can have fire drills.

CHAPTER 7

Staying Safe

Reading Skill

Find the Main Idea

The main idea of something you are reading is what it is mostly about. The details tell more about it.

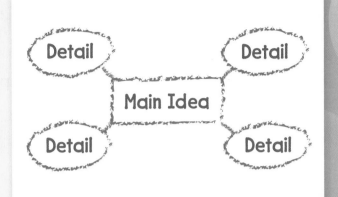

Health Graph

Daily Physical Activity

You should exercise every day. Avoid danger by never exercising alone.

 Be Active!

Use **Movin' and Groovin'** on Track 7.

Staying Safe Around Water

Lesson Focus
You can stay safe around water.

Swimming is a good way to get exercise. It is also fun! But you need to be careful around water.

The best way to be safe is to learn how to swim. Never go into the water alone. Make sure a parent or another trusted adult is watching you. Always obey water safety rules.

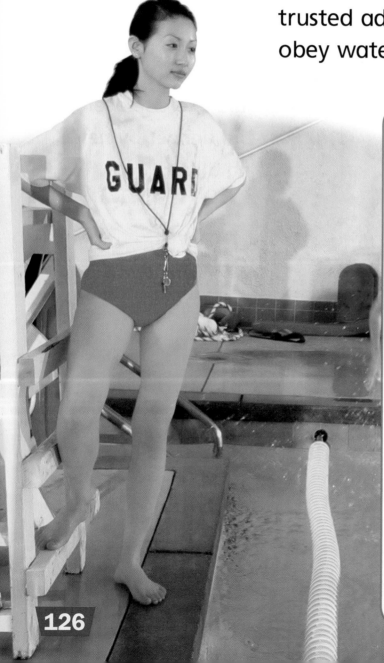

Water Safety Rules

► Learn how to swim.

► Never swim alone.

► Do not push others into the water.

► Do not chew gum or eat in the water.

► Get out of the water if there is lightning or thunder.

► Find out how deep the water is before you jump or dive in.

► Do not swim if you are tired.

► Do not swim in the dark.

You can stay safe in a boat. Never go in a boat without an adult. Before you go, talk about what to do if an emergency happens. Always wear a life jacket. It will help you float if you fall out of the boat.

If it looks as if a storm is coming, go back to shore. A boat is not a safe place to be in a storm.

Review

1 How can you stay safe around water?

2 What are four water safety rules?

3 Write about how to stay safe in a boat.

Staying Safe Around Animals

Lesson Focus
You can stay safe around animals.

It is fun to see animals if you know how to stay safe around them.

Never bother an animal when it is eating, drinking, or sleeping. Do not tease or pull on an animal. This can scare it. Loud noises or sudden moves can also scare an animal. Then it may bite or scratch you.

Stay away from animals you do not know and from all wild animals.

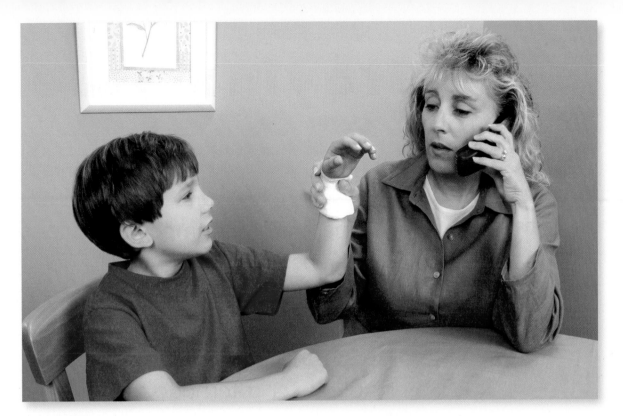

If an animal bites or scratches you, tell a trusted adult right away. If you know the animal, the adult can tell the animal's owner what happened.

If your skin is broken, an adult should wash the bite or scratch with soap. The adult should also call a doctor. A bite or scratch needs special care. The doctor will explain what to do.

Review

1 Why should you be careful around animals?

2 Name four ways to stay safe around animals.

3 Write about what to do if an animal bites or scratches you.

Staying Safe at School

Lesson Focus

School rules help you stay safe.

Your school has rules to keep you safe. There are very important rules to follow if there is a fire in the school. You have fire drills to practice what to do. Your school may also practice what to do in other emergencies, such as an earthquake or a tornado.

There are also rules to keep you safe on the playground. Do not push. Wait for your turn. Do not walk too close to the swings.

How are these children following playground safety rules?

If you hurt yourself or you do not feel well, tell your teacher. You may need help from the school nurse or another adult. The adult will call your parents or another adult family member.

You need to get help if you are choking. What is this boy learning to do to help him stay safe?

How to get help if you choke

Review

1 Why should you follow school rules?

2 What should you do if you feel ill at school?

3 Write a list of rules that keep you safe on the playground. Tell why they are important.

Resolve Conflicts

People have conflicts sometimes. A **conflict** is a disagreement. People can **resolve**, or settle, their conflicts in peaceful ways. These steps show how.

1 **Agree that there is a problem.**

> You have to move. My friend and I always sit here.

In the lunchroom, Nia tells Laura and Rosa they have taken her table. She and her friend want to sit there.

2 **Listen to one another.**

> We got here first.

> There are no empty tables.

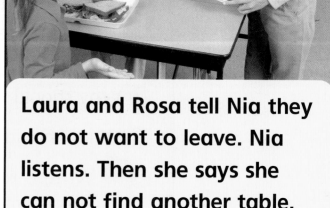

Laura and Rosa tell Nia they do not want to leave. Nia listens. Then she says she can not find another table.

3 Think of ways to work together.

We can all sit here.

There is room for four at the table. Rosa invites Nia to sit with them.

4 Find a way for both sides to win.

Nia thanks them and sits down. When Nia's friend comes, the four girls share the table.

Problem Solving

Use the steps to solve this problem.

You and a friend are playing with a ball. An older boy comes over to you. He wants the ball. He tells you to give it to him. How can you resolve this conflict?

Staying Safe on Wheels

Follow these rules to ride a bike safely.

▶ Obey all traffic laws and signs.

▶ Walk the bike when you cross streets. Use crosswalks. Do what crossing guards tell you to do.

▶ Always ride in single file.

▶ Keep both hands on the handlebar. Do not carry things in your hands or wear a backpack. Use the bike's basket.

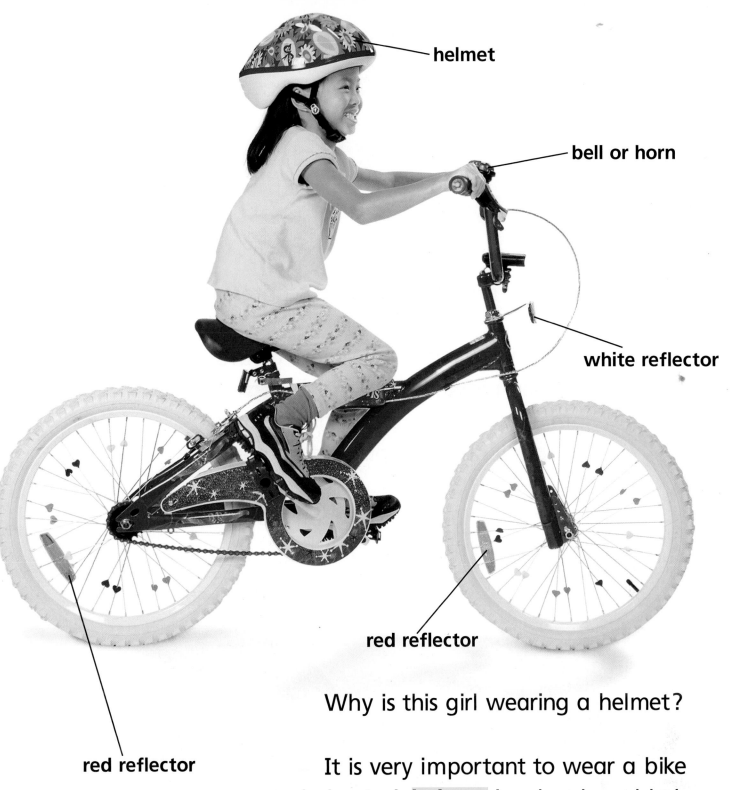

helmet

bell or horn

white reflector

red reflector

red reflector

Why is this girl wearing a helmet?

It is very important to wear a bike helmet. A **helmet** is a hard, padded hat that protects the head. It is also important to have the right gear on your bike. It should have a bell or a horn. It should also have reflectors.

Skates, skateboards, and scooters are fun to use. But if you fall, you can get an **injury**, or get hurt. Wearing safety gear can protect you. **Safety gear** is clothing and other things that protect your body and help prevent injuries.

How does this safety gear protect your body and prevent injuries?

knee pad

elbow pad

mouth guard

Learn how to fall safely by landing on the soft parts of your body. Also, roll instead of putting out your arms to stop yourself. Doing these things will help you keep from hurting yourself.

Use skates, skateboards, and scooters only on smooth ground. Never use them near traffic or at night.

helmet

wrist guard

Review

1 **Vocabulary** Why is **safety gear** important?

2 Make a poster that shows how to protect your body when you use skates or a scooter.

3 Write a list of five things you can do to ride a bike safely.

Staying Safe in a Car or Bus

A person who rides in a car or bus is called a **passenger**. A passenger in a car should always wear a safety belt. A **safety belt** is a strap that holds you safely in a seat. It will help protect you if there is a crash or a fast stop.

Children should sit in the back seat of a car. Children who are less than nine years old should also use booster seats. A booster seat makes the safety belt fit correctly.

Always keep your head, hands, and feet inside a car. Do not play with anything that is sharp or pointed. Sit quietly so that the driver can pay attention to the traffic.

To be safe when you get onto a bus, wait in a line until the bus stops. Do not wait too close to the street.

The bus driver will tell you when it is safe to get onto the bus. Be careful as you get on. Do not push on the steps. Do not rush to get a seat.

You can be a safe passenger in a bus. Wear a safety belt if there is one. Do not play with sharp or pointed objects. Sit quietly, and keep your head and hands inside.

Be careful as you get off the bus. Never walk behind the bus after you get off.

Review

1. **Vocabulary** Why is a **safety belt** important?

2. How can you get onto a bus safely?

3. Write three things you can do to ride safely in cars and buses.

ACTIVITIES

Math

Pet Graph

How many children have cats?

How many have rabbits?

How many children in all have rabbits and fish?

Make your own graph about pets.

Writing

Make a Safety Book

Explain how to stay safe around water. Draw pictures that show what to do. Write a sentence for each picture. Use your pictures to make a water safety book.

 For more activities, visit The Learning Site.
www.harcourtschool.com/health

Citizenship

Showing Good Citizenship

When you help keep yourself and others in your neighborhood safe, you show good citizenship. Good **citizenship** is being a good citizen, or member, of a community.

Show good citizenship where you live. Follow rules for keeping your community safe. Help others do the same.

How are these children showing good citizenship?

Activity

List some ways you show good citizenship by following safety rules where you live.

143

Chapter Review

Use Health Words

Tell which picture goes best with the word or words.

a.   **b.**

1 **helmet**

2 **safety belt**

3 **passengers**

4 **safety gear**

c.   **d.**

 Reading Skill

5 Tell the main idea.

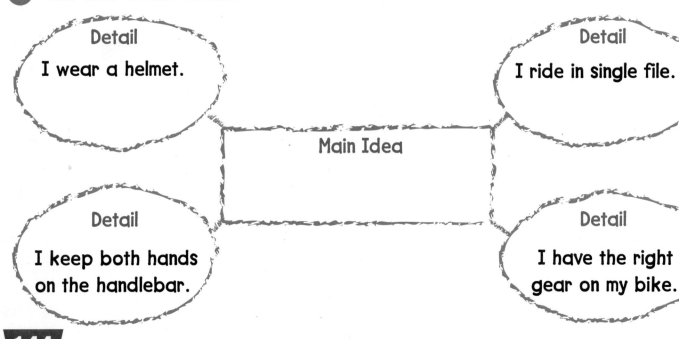

Detail
I wear a helmet.

Detail
I ride in single file.

Main Idea

Detail
I keep both hands on the handlebar.

Detail
I have the right gear on my bike.

Use Life Skills

Look at the pictures. Then answer the questions.

a.

b.

6 Which picture shows how the children resolve the conflict?

7 What are four steps you can use to resolve conflicts?

Write About It

8 Write about someone at your school who helps you stay safe. Tell how this person can help you.

My coach can show me how to wear safety gear.

Make Predictions

When you make a prediction, you tell what you think will happen next.

Prediction

What Happened

Health Graph

Days We Were Ill

1 day	👤👤👤👤
2 days	👤👤
3 days	👤👤
4 days	👤👤👤
5 days	👤

Key: Each 👤 stands for 2 children.

Daily Physical Activity

Exercise every day to help your body stay well.

 Be Active!

Use **Jumping and Pumping** on Track 8.

Feeling Ill

Lesson Focus
You do not feel well when you are ill.

Vocabulary
ill

When you are **ill**, you are not well. Your body feels different. You may have a sore throat, runny nose, fever, or rash. You may feel tired, and parts of your body may hurt.

Tell an adult family member or your teacher if you feel ill. Tell where you hurt and whether you feel hot or cold.

digital ear thermometer

Your parent or another trusted adult will help you get well. He or she may tell you to rest. Rest helps your body get stronger. He or she may give you something to make you feel better.

You may need to see a doctor. He or she can find out why you are ill. Then the doctor can tell your parent how to help you get better.

Review

1 **Vocabulary** How can you tell if you are **ill**?

2 Name two things you can do to get better.

3 Write about how people may feel if they are ill.

Communicate

When you are ill, you need help. Find an adult you trust. Then **communicate**, or tell, how you feel so you can get help. These steps show how.

1 **Choose an adult to talk to.**

Pedro is trying to play baseball, but he is coughing a lot. Pedro wants to ask his coach for help.

2 **Say what you need to say.**

I have a bad cough.

Pedro finds his coach. He tells his coach about his coughing.

3 Listen carefully.
Answer any questions.

Are you feeling ill in any other way?

Yes. My chest hurts.

The coach asks questions to find out more about how Pedro feels. Pedro answers him clearly.

4 Get information.

Pedro has adult family members at the game. The coach will find them. They will tell Pedro what to do to feel better.

 Problem Solving

Use the steps to solve this problem.

You are playing in your backyard. Suddenly your leg feels itchy. You see a rash on it. Who can help you? What should you say about how you feel?

Preventing Illness

Lesson Focus
Keeping germs
from spreading
helps you stay
healthy.

Vocabulary
disease
germs
vaccine

You may have a disease if you are ill. A **disease** is a kind of illness. **Germs** are tiny things that can cause some diseases. Colds and flu are caused by germs called viruses. Other diseases are caused by germs called bacteria.

Germs spread from person to person. They spread through the air when people sneeze or cough. If the germs get into your body, they can give you an illness.

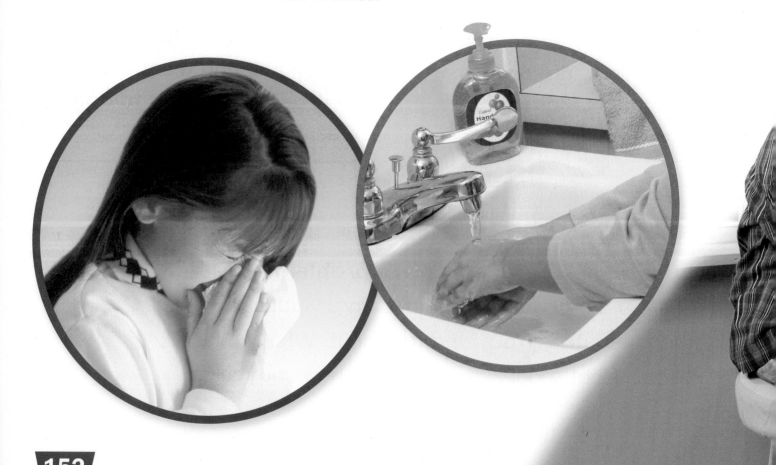

You can help stop germs from spreading.

▶ Cover your mouth and nose when you sneeze or cough. Wash your hands with soap and warm water afterwards.

▶ Use a tissue to blow your nose. Throw the tissue away. Then wash your hands.

▶ Do not get close to people with colds.

▶ Stay at home if you have an illness that can spread.

▶ Do not share cups, straws, forks, or any other things you put in your mouth.

Your body protects you from disease. Your skin keeps germs from getting inside your body. If you cut your skin, put on a plastic bandage to keep out germs.

The tears in your eyes wash out germs. Mucus in your nose keeps germs from getting into your lungs.

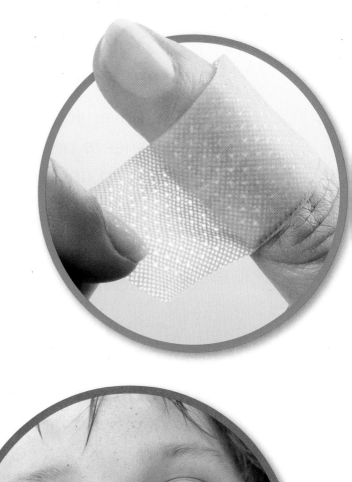

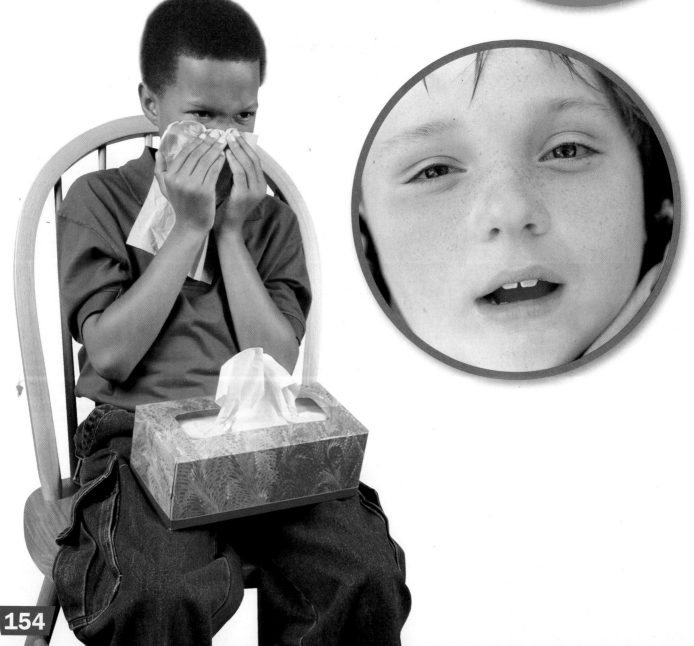

A **vaccine** protects you from getting a disease. It helps your body fight off the germs that cause the disease. You get most vaccines as shots. There are vaccines to protect you from measles, mumps, chicken pox, and other diseases.

Regular checkups also keep you from becoming ill. They make sure you are healthy. Health checks at school can find health problems early.

Review

1 **Vocabulary** What is a **vaccine**?

2 How does your body protect you?

3 Write about the ways germs spread and what you can do to stop them.

Illnesses That Do Not Spread

Lesson Focus
Some illnesses do not spread from person to person.

Vocabulary
allergy
asthma

Some illnesses are not caused by germs. They do not spread from person to person. An **allergy** is an illness that does not spread. It is not caused by germs. It happens when people eat a certain food or are near or touch a certain plant or animal.

Some people who have an allergy get a rash or feel itchy. Others may sneeze a lot. They may also have a runny nose, itchy eyes, and a sore throat. This kind of allergy feels like a cold.

If you have an allergy, stay away from the thing that makes you ill. An adult family member can give you something to help you feel better.

Asthma is an illness that is not caused by germs and does not spread. Smoke, furry animals, and other things may make it hard for someone who has asthma to breathe.

When people with asthma have trouble breathing, they may use something to help them. A child with asthma can get help from a family member, a teacher, or the school nurse.

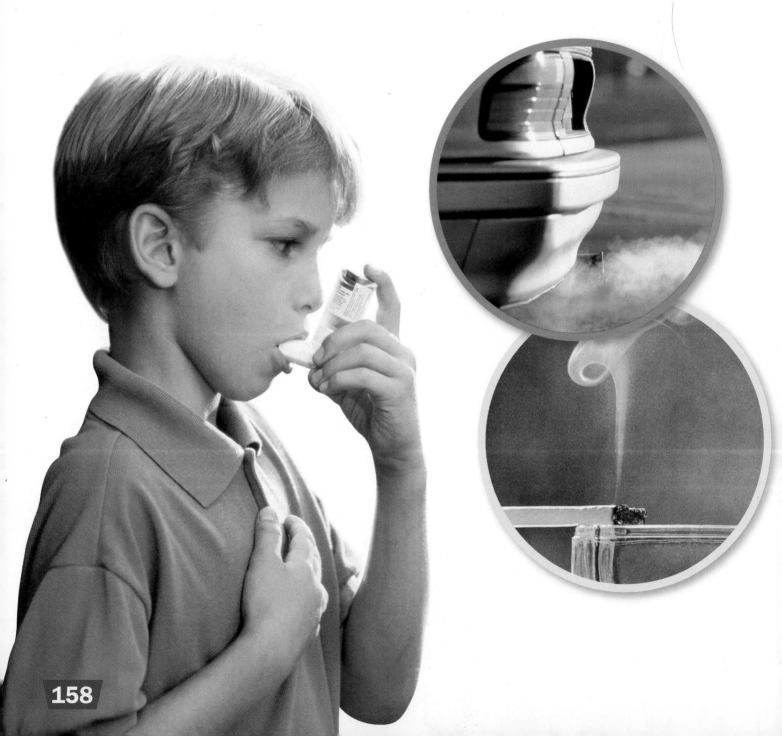

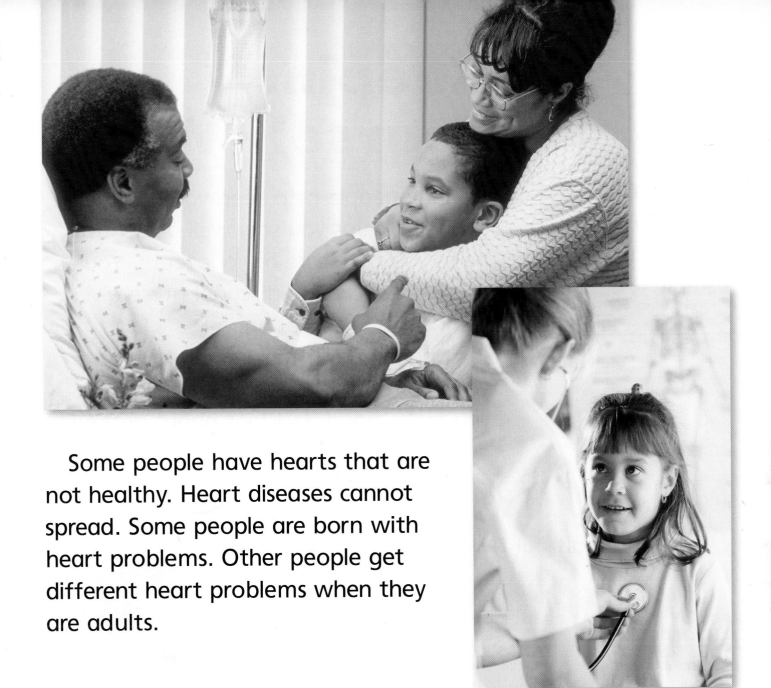

Some people have hearts that are not healthy. Heart diseases cannot spread. Some people are born with heart problems. Other people get different heart problems when they are adults.

Review

1. **Vocabulary** What is an **allergy**?

2. Name three things that can cause a person with an allergy to become ill.

3. Write about people you can tell if someone at school is having trouble breathing.

Keeping Yourself Well

Lesson Focus
You can help yourself stay healthy.

Many people help keep you healthy. A doctor helps you stay well. A dentist helps you take care of your teeth. Your parents, teacher, and school nurse give you health information.

At home, adult family members give you healthful foods to eat. They help you make good decisions about getting enough exercise and rest.

Eat healthful foods.

Get enough rest.

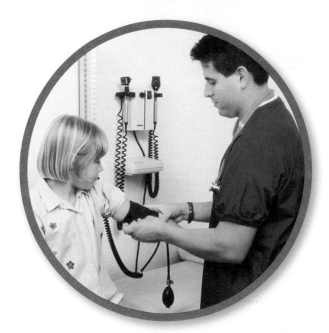

Who else can help you stay well? You can! You can keep your body clean. You can eat the right foods. You can get enough exercise, rest, and sleep. All these things help keep you healthy and strong.

See a doctor and a dentist for regular checkups. Follow their instructions.

Keep yourself clean.

Get lots of exercise.

Review

1 Who can help you stay healthy? Tell how.

2 How can your family help you stay healthy?

3 Write about things you should and should not do to stay healthy.

ACTIVITIES

Math

Allergies Graph

How many children have allergies to pets?

How many children in all have allergies?

Make your own graph about allergies.

Writing

Get-Well Card

Make a get-well card for someone who is ill. Draw a picture on the front. Inside, write sentences to tell the person you hope he or she feels better.

GO For more activities, visit The Learning Site.
ONLINE www.harcourtschool.com/health

Caring

Being Caring to People with Health Needs

Some people have illnesses or injuries that will not go away. They may have special health needs. You can be **caring** to people with health needs. Ask if you can help them with chores. Invite them to do things with you and your friends. Show respect for them.

How is this boy being caring?

Activity

Write a letter to someone with special health needs. Ask how you can help him or her.

163

Use Health Words

Tell which picture goes best with the word.

1 ill

2 vaccine

3 asthma

4 allergy

a.

b.

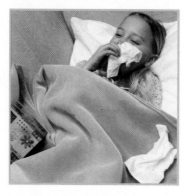

c.

d

Focus Skill Reading Skill

5 Jimmy does not get enough sleep.
Predict what will happen.

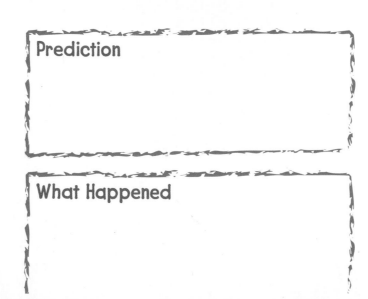

Prediction

What Happened

Use Life Skills

Look at the picture. Then answer the questions.

6 What should you do if you feel ill when you are not at home?

7 What are four steps you can use to communicate when you feel ill?

Write About It

8 Write about some things you can do to keep germs from spreading.

I can cover my mouth when I cough.

Medicines and Drugs

Reading Skill

Use Context Clues

The words, pictures, and charts near a new word can help you understand it.

Clues

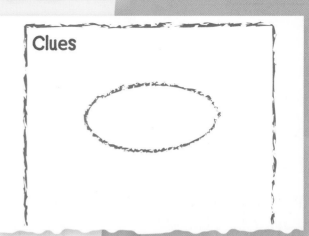

Health Graph

Ads for Medicines

Medicines						
cough medicines						
pain relievers						
cold medicines						

0 1 2 3 4 5 6
Number of Ads

Daily Physical Activity

Say NO to drugs to help keep your body healthy. Exercise to help it stay healthy, too.

 **Be Active!**

Use **Hop To It** on Track 9.

Using Medicines Safely

Lesson Focus
Medicines can help you when you use them safely.

Vocabulary
prescription medicines

over-the-counter medicines

You may need medicines when you are ill or hurt. Some medicines make you feel better and help you get well. Other medicines help you stay healthy.

Some medicines are pills or liquids that you swallow. Others are creams that you rub on your skin. Some medicines are given as shots.

Use medicines safely. Don't take any medicines without first asking your parents. Never play with medicines. They should always be kept in a locked cabinet.

Medicines that doctors order for you are called **prescription medicines**. Use only as much as the doctor tells you to. Taking too much can hurt you. Never take another person's medicine. Medicines can be harmful if they are used in wrong ways. A trusted adult will help you take medicines safely.

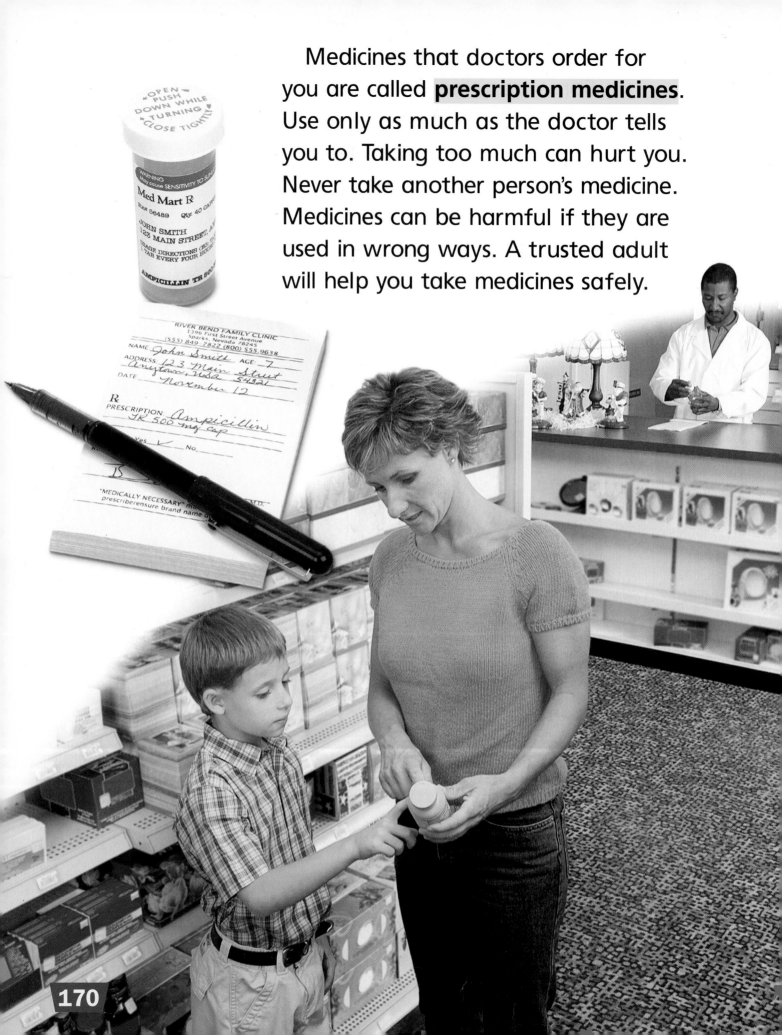

Adults can get some medicines without a doctor's order. These are called **over-the-counter medicines**.

People need to read the labels on medicines carefully. Labels tell what the medicines do. They tell how much to take and when to take it. Labels also give warnings about ways the medicines could be harmful.

What can you learn from this label?

Review

1 **Vocabulary** What is the difference between **over-the-counter medicines** and **prescription medicines**?

2 How can medicines help you?

3 Write rules for using medicines safely.

Drugs

Drugs change the way your body works. Medicines are helpful drugs.

Other drugs can harm you. Beer and wine have a harmful drug in them. Cigarettes and other kinds of tobacco have a harmful drug, too. These drugs are NOT medicines.

Chocolate, some kinds of coffee and tea, and some soft drinks also contain a drug. This drug is not good for you if you get too much of it.

Lesson Focus
Medicines used safely can help you, but other drugs can harm you.

Vocabulary
drugs

Saying NO to harmful drugs protects your body and keeps you safe.

Drugs can make it hard to think clearly. Then you might make bad decisions.

Drugs can make you want to hurt people.

Drugs can stop your body from growing.

Review

① **Vocabulary** What is a **drug**?

② Which things on the page are helpful medicines? Which things contain harmful drugs?

③ Write about the differences between medicines and other drugs.

173

Caffeine

Caffeine is a drug. It changes the way the body works. Tea, coffee, chocolate, and soft drinks may contain caffeine.

Some products have caffeine even though it is not listed on the label. Others have the caffeine taken out. These products are "caffeine free."

Some people have a habit of using caffeine. A **habit** is something a person does often. Someone with a caffeine habit drinks caffeine drinks instead of more healthful drinks. Too much caffeine can make your heart beat fast and make you feel nervous. Caffeine can make it hard to sleep.

Review

1 **Vocabulary** What is **caffeine**, and what foods and drinks contain it?

2 How can having caffeine become a habit?

3 Write about why you might choose foods and drinks without caffeine.

Tobacco and Alcohol

Tobacco is a plant. Some people smoke it in cigarettes, cigars, and pipes. Some people chew tobacco.

Tobacco contains a drug called **nicotine**. When people smoke or chew tobacco, they get nicotine in their bodies. The nicotine makes it very hard for people who use tobacco to stop using it. A tobacco habit is very harmful to health.

Tobacco has many other harmful drugs besides nicotine. When tobacco burns, it makes **tobacco smoke**. People who smoke tobacco or breathe someone else's smoke get these harmful drugs in their bodies. People who chew tobacco get these drugs in their bodies, too.

The drugs in tobacco can cause heart problems, cancer, and other diseases that often lead to death.

Tobacco can cause lung cancer.

Tobacco can cause heart disease.

Tobacco can make it hard to breathe.

Alcohol can be a harmful drug. Beer, wine, and liquor are drinks that contain alcohol. Too much alcohol can act like a poison to many parts of the body. It can even cause death.

Alcohol slows down the brain. It makes it hard to think clearly. It can cause people to make bad decisions.

Alcohol can hurt the heart and liver.

Alcohol can make it hard for the body to fight diseases.

Alcohol can stop bones and muscles from growing well.

Warning– Can be dangerous. May cause health problems. Not for use by children.

Alcohol can change people's moods. It can make them feel angry or sad. It can make them act silly or behave unsafely.

It is against the law for children and teenagers to buy or drink alcohol. It is also against the law for adults to drink too much alcohol and drive. They can cause bad crashes that cause injuries and deaths.

Review

1 **Vocabulary** What is **tobacco**?

2 How can alcohol harm your body?

3 Make a poster about saying NO to tobacco and alcohol use.

Refusing Drugs

Lesson Focus
Saying NO to drugs will keep you safe and healthy.

Vocabulary
self-control

Some people may try to get you to use drugs. They may dare you to try them. They may say using drugs will make you feel like an adult. Do not trust people who say this. They do not care about your health.

Some ads try to make you think drugs are fun and safe to use. Do not believe these ads. Remember that drugs can hurt you badly.

To refuse drugs is to say NO to them. Do not touch or pick up any drugs. Tell a trusted adult that you saw drugs. Tell where they are.

Refusing to touch or use drugs takes self-control. You show **self-control** when you control your actions by making good decisions.

It can help to practice saying NO. An adult family member, a teacher, or a police officer can help you plan ways to say NO to drugs.

Review

1 **Vocabulary** What is **self-control**?

2 How do ads trick people into trying drugs?

3 Write a list of ways to refuse drugs.

LIFE SKILLS

Refuse to Use Drugs

People who use drugs may ask you to use drugs, too. Here is what you can do to **refuse**, or say NO to, drugs.

1 **Say NO.**

Jeff offers a cigarette to Marco. Marco says NO and does not take the cigarette.

2 **Give a reason.**

Marco tells Jeff that tobacco is very bad for a person's health.

3 **Say NO again.**

I said NO! It's bad for me!

Jeff keeps trying to get Marco to smoke. Marco refuses again.

4 **Tell a trusted adult.**

Marco tells his mom that he refused Jeff's cigarette. Marco's mom says he did the right thing.

 # Problem Solving

Use the steps to solve this problem.

You are playing at a friend's house. Your friend finds a beer can. It has some beer left in it. She asks if you want to taste the beer. How will you refuse?

ACTIVITIES

Math

Caffeine-Free Graph

How many children chose milk?

Which two drinks did the same number of children choose?

Make your own graph about caffeine-free drinks.

Writing

A Rhyme

Write a rhyme. It should tell children to get help from parents or other trusted adults when they take medicine. Put your rhyme on a poster. Put it up in the classroom.

Talk to Mom and Dad if you feel bad.

 For more activities, visit The Learning Site.
www.harcourtschool.com/health

Responsibility

Practicing Self-Control

You show **responsibility** when you refuse to use drugs. It takes self-control to do this. When you have self-control, you make good decisions and can stop yourself from doing harmful things.

Use self-control about medicines, too. Do not take them on your own when you feel sick. Always take medicines with help from a parent or another trusted adult.

How is this girl showing self-control?

Activity

Suppose you feel sick. A friend wants to give you some of her medicine. What will you do? Work with a partner. Act out what you would say to each other.

Chapter Review

Use Health Words

Use the words to tell about the pictures.

1 nicotine

2 prescription medicines

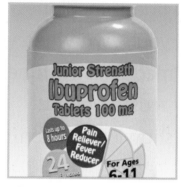

3 over-the-counter medicines

4 caffeine

(Focus Skill) Reading Skill

5 Read the clues in the box. Use them to figure out the word that belongs in the center.

Clues

It burns when people smoke it.

Tobacco

It is used to make cigarettes.

Breathing it is harmful.

Use Life Skills

Look at the picture. Then answer the questions.

6 What is one reason you can give for refusing drugs? *It can hurt my body.*

7 What are four steps you can follow to refuse drugs? *Say no, give reasoany say no again, Tell adult.*

Write About It

8 Write about some ways alcohol can harm your body.

Drinking alcohol can hurt my brain.

CHAPTER 10

Your Feelings

ME

Reading Skill

Recall and Retell

To recall is to remember what you have read. To retell is to tell it in your own words.

Recall Detail	Retell
Recall Detail	
Recall Detail	

Health Graph

Activities We Do with Parents

Activities				
play games				
make snacks				
watch movies				
read books				

0   3   6   9   12

Number of Children

Daily Physical Activity

If you feel sad or angry, exercise can help you feel better. Exercise every day.

Be Active!

Use **Super Stress Buster** on Track 10.

People Are Special

You are special. Being **special** is being different from everyone else. No one acts and feels just the way you do. No one looks just like you.

All people are special. They look different. Their feelings are different. They act in different ways, too.

All people feel happy and sad. But they may have these feelings at different times and for different reasons. They show their feelings in different ways.

People learn in different ways. They also want to learn about different things. They have different interests.

People have different skills and like to do different things. Some like to dance or play music. Others like to read or play sports. Some people like to do all of these things.

What do these children like to do?

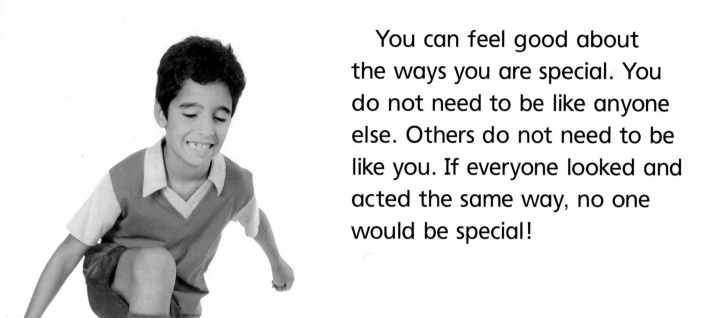

You can feel good about the ways you are special. You do not need to be like anyone else. Others do not need to be like you. If everyone looked and acted the same way, no one would be special!

Review

1 **Vocabulary** What is being **special**?

2 Name four ways each person is special.

3 Write about ways you are special.

Managing Your Feelings

Lesson Focus
It is important to know how to manage your feelings.

Vocabulary
needs
wants
emotions
self-control

Needs are things you must have, such as food, water, and shelter. You also need love, a place to belong, and a trusted adult to care for you. **Wants** are things you would like to have but do not need. Needs should be met before wants.

One of these boys is ready to go swimming. His brother is ill. Which boy has a need? Which boy has a want?

You can tell the adults who care for you about your needs and wants. Speak calmly. Do not yell. Trust your adults to do what is best for you.

If you do not get what you want, you may feel sad or angry. Sadness and anger are **emotions**, or feelings. So are happiness, fear, and worry. Share your emotions calmly. Your family will help you with them.

Everyone feels sad or lonely at some time. Here are some ways you can help yourself feel better.

► Think about why you feel as you do.

► Write about how you feel. Draw pictures to show how you feel.

► Talk to your family about your feelings.

Having **self-control** is controlling your emotions and actions. Practice self-control when you are angry. Instead of shouting, hitting, or throwing things, use these tips.

► Think about why you are angry.

► Take some time to calm down.

► Think of a way to feel better.

Review

1 **Vocabulary** What is having **self-control**?

2 Name three things you can do to keep control when you are angry.

3 Write a letter to tell a friend how to feel better when he or she is sad or upset.

Manage Stress

Going to school can sometimes give you **stress**, or nervous feelings. You can learn how to manage, or deal with, your stress. Here is what you can do.

1 Know what stress feels like.

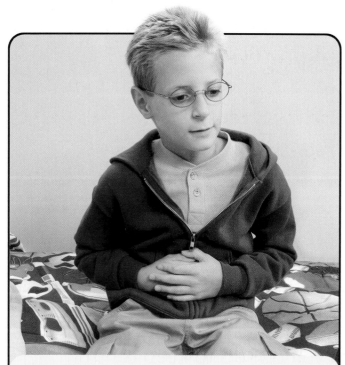

Max is feeling stress. The stress is making his stomach hurt.

2 Figure out why you feel stress.

Max must give a report in class tomorrow. He is worried that he will not do a good job. Other children may laugh at him.

3 **Do something to feel better. Talk to someone you trust.**

4 **Prepare so you can manage the stress.**

Don't worry. You'll do a great job.

Thanks, Mom. I feel better now.

Max talks to his mom about his stress. She listens and helps calm him.

Max practices giving his report in front of his mom. He feels ready to give his report tomorrow.

 Problem Solving

Use the steps to solve this problem.

You have a big spelling test tomorrow. You feel stress because you do not think you are ready for it. How can you manage your stress?

Being Responsible

Lesson Focus
You are responsible to your family, your friends, your community, and yourself.

Vocabulary
responsible

If you are **responsible**, people can count on you. Your friends know you can be trusted. Your family members know you do what you are supposed to do. No one needs to remind you to follow rules and help out at home.

You are responsible to your school. You follow school rules. You listen to your teacher.

You are also responsible to your community. You help keep it safe and clean. You obey laws and rules.

You are responsible to yourself, too. You learn things that will help you. You keep yourself safe and healthy. You stand up for what is right.

Review

1. **Vocabulary** What is being **responsible**?

2. How are you responsible to your community and to yourself?

3. Write about why it is important to be responsible to your family and friends.

Showing Respect

Lesson Focus

Showing respect helps you get along with people.

Vocabulary

respect

Knowing how to get along with people is important. One way to do this is to show respect for them. You show **respect** when you act and talk politely. You say "please," "thank you," and "you're welcome." You do not yell or talk when someone else is talking.

Are these children showing respect?

Are these children showing respect?

You also show respect when you share and work with others. You are kind and helpful. You listen carefully to people. You raise your hand to get your teacher's attention.

Review

❶ **Vocabulary** How do you show **respect**?

❷ Why is showing respect important?

❸ Write two lists. Tell ways the children in the pictures are and are not showing respect.

Being a Friend

A friend is someone you can trust. Friends like to do things together. They listen to each other and share their feelings. They like to play together.

You can make a new friend. Try asking someone new to play a game or sit with you at lunch.

Friends teach each other how to do new things. They also show respect for each other. A good friend does not ask you to do something that is wrong or unsafe. A good friend helps you stay healthy and safe.

Review

1 Name three things friends do together.

2 How can you make a new friend?

3 ✏ Write about ways friends act with each other.

ACTIVITIES

Math

Ways to Relax Graph

How many children chose listening to music?

How many more chose painting than exercising?

Make your own graph about ways to relax and manage stress.

Ways We Like to Relax

exercise	😊 😊 😊
listen to music	😊 😊
paint pictures	😊 😊 😊 😊

Key: Each 😊 stands for 3 children.

Writing

Happy Poem

Think of things that make you happy. Write a short poem about them. Then share it with the class.

Happy Poem

I love to play outside.
I go down the slide.

 GO ONLINE For more activities, visit The Learning Site.
www.harcourtschool.com/health

Respect

Showing Respect by Including Everyone

You can show **respect** by including everyone in a game or an activity. Sometimes a person may not be able to do an activity the way you usually do it. If you adapt, or change, the activity, everyone can join in.

How are these children showing respect for one another?

Activity

Work with a partner. List ways you can include everyone in a game or an activity.

207

Chapter Review

Use Health Words

Use the word to tell about the picture.

1 special

2 responsible

3 respect

4 emotions

Focus Skill Reading Skill

5 Retell what you learned about being a good friend.

Recall Detail	Retell
A friend is someone you can trust.	
Recall Detail	
Friends share their feelings.	
Recall Detail	
Friends learn from each other.	

Use Life Skills

Look at the picture. Then answer the questions.

6 How does Max know he is feeling stress?

7 What are four steps you can use to manage stress?

Write About It

8 Write about some ways you can be responsible at home.

I can be responsible by keeping my room clean.

CHAPTER 11

Your Family

Recall and Retell

To recall is to remember what you have read. To retell is to tell it in your own words.

Recall Detail	Retell
Recall Detail	
Recall Detail	

Health Graph

Activities Liked When Adults Were Children

Activities:
- playing sports
- dancing
- painting
- reading

0 3 6 9 12
Number of People

Daily Physical Activity

You should exercise every day. The people in your family can exercise together.

 **Be Active!**

Use **Funky Flex** on Track 11.

Families

Lesson Focus
People in a
family love and
care for one
another.

Vocabulary
love

A family is made up of people who care about one another. Every family is different and special. Parents, sisters, brothers, grandparents, and others can all be members of a family.

Family members love one another. **Love** is a special feeling of caring for someone. Family members show their love for one another in many ways.

People in a family take care of one another. They help when a family member is ill or has a problem. Family members work and play together. They teach one another. They share holidays and other special days.

Review

1. **Vocabulary** What is **love**?

2. How do people in a family take care of one another?

3. Draw and write about some things family members do together.

Getting Along with Family Members

Lesson Focus
Family members get along when they help and respect one another.

Vocabulary
chores

Your family helps you. You can help your family, too. One way to help is to do your share of chores. **Chores** are jobs you do to help at home. What chores are these children doing?

You can get along with family members the same way you get along with other people. Be polite and kind. Show respect. Do not make fun of anyone.

215

Most families have rules. Some of these rules help family members get along. Here are some rules that help people get along.

► Take turns.

► Share.

► Speak politely.

► Ask before you borrow something.

Your family may have other rules, too.

Family members get along when they work together. If they do not agree, they talk and listen with respect. They have fun together. How are these family members getting along?

Review

1 **Vocabulary** Draw three pictures of children doing **chores** at home.

2 Why are family rules important?

3 Write about things people in a family can do to show they respect one another.

Resolve Conflicts

People have **conflicts** when they do not agree. Conflicts can happen in families for many reasons. Members of a family can **resolve**, or settle, conflicts. How can you help resolve your family conflicts?

1 **Agree that there is a problem.**

Jan wants to use her sister's batteries. Cara does not want to lend them to Jan.

2 **Listen to each other.**

The girls talk. Cara wants to save her batteries. Jan says she needs them for her flashlight.

3 Work together to reach an agreement.

Jan says she will buy Cara new batteries later. Cara agrees to let Jan use her batteries now.

4 Find a way for both sides to win.

Jan and Cara are both glad they resolved the conflict.

 Problem Solving

Use the steps to solve this problem.

You and your brother are eating pizza for lunch. Now only one slice is left. You both reach for it at the same time. How can you and your brother resolve this conflict?

Families Change

Families go through many kinds of changes. Some changes are happy. Other changes are sad.

Losing a pet or a person you love is one kind of change. If someone dies, you may feel sad and upset. Share your feelings with a family member. This may help both of you feel better.

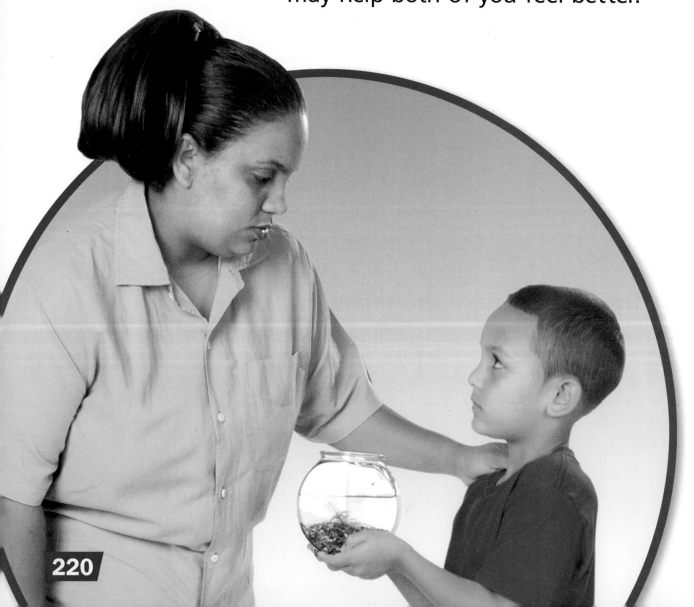

HOUSE
FOR SALE
SOLD

Sarah's Room

Moving to a new home is another kind of change. Leaving your home may be hard. You have to leave your friends and go to a new school. You will make new friends. You can still talk to your old friends, too.

Some parents get a divorce. After two people get a **divorce**, they are not married any more. People are often sad about a divorce. Children should tell their parents how they feel. After a divorce, children still have a family. They can still have fun with family members.

Having a new brother or sister can be fun, but you have to share your parents' time. It takes a while to get used to having a new person in the family.

All families go through changes. These changes affect everyone in the family. No matter how your family changes, you are an important part of it. You and the other members of your family still love and care for one another.

Review

1. **Vocabulary** What is a **divorce**?

2. Why is it important to share your feelings when you feel sad or upset?

3. Write about three ways families can change.

ACTIVITIES

Math

Family Chores Graph

How many children sweep the floor?

How many more children wipe the table than feed pets?

Make a graph about family chores.

Our Chores at Home

wipe table	🖐	🖐	🖐	
sweep floors	🖐			
feed pets	🖐	🖐		
clean our rooms	🖐	🖐	🖐	🖐

Key: Each 🖐 stands for 3 children.

Writing

Puppet Stories

Read a story about a family that deals with a change. Make a puppet of one character. Write what the character would say about his or her feelings. Use the puppet to share the feelings with the class.

 For more activities, visit The Learning Site.
www.harcourtschool.com/health

Fairness

Being Fair About Your Mistakes

People sometimes make mistakes. You may want to hide a mistake. You may even want to say that your brother or sister made the mistake.

It is important to tell your parents if you break something or make another mistake. It is not **fair**, or right, to say that someone else made the mistake. When people see that you tell the truth about your mistakes, they will trust you. They will know that you are fair.

How is this boy being fair?

Activity

Role-play a scene in which someone tells about a mistake he or she has made.

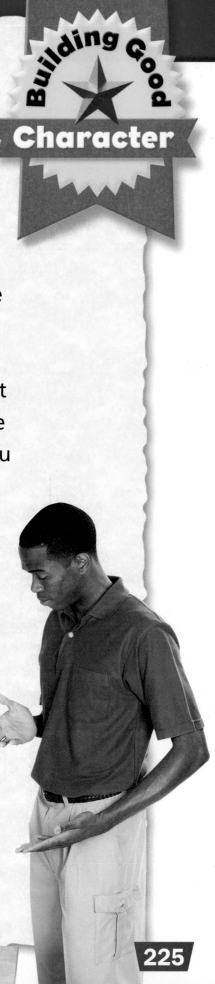

Chapter Review

Use Health Words

Use the word to tell about the picture.

1 love

2 chores

3 conflict

4 resolve

Focus Skill Reading Skill

5 Recall and retell what you learned about families.

Recall Detail	Retell
People in a family respect one another.	
Recall Detail Family members work and play together.	
Recall Detail Family members share special days.	

Use Life Skills

Look at the pictures. Then answer the questions.

6 Which picture shows the better way to resolve a conflict?

7 What are four steps that can help you resolve conflicts?

Write About It

8 Write about ways people in a family can take care of one another.

A Family
A dad can cook for the family. A brother sometimes helps with homework.

12 Caring for Your Neighborhood

Reading Skill

Find Cause and Effect

An effect is something that happens. A cause is the reason something happens.

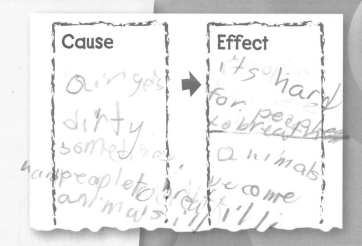

Cause	Effect
air gets dirty sometimes make people dirty animals	it's so hard for people to breathe animals become ill

Health Graph

Pounds of Cans We Recycled

Number of Pounds

12 11 10 9 8 7 6 5 4 3 2 1 0

January   February   March   April

Months

Daily Physical Activity

You should exercise every day. Find places in your community where you can exercise safely.

 Be Active!

Use **Broadway Bound** on Track 12.

Your School

Many people at school help you stay healthy and safe. Your teachers tell you ways to take care of yourself. They show you ways to exercise and stay fit.

A school librarian can help you learn about being healthy. The librarian can help you find books and magazines with health information. The librarian or a teacher can help you find health information on the Internet, too.

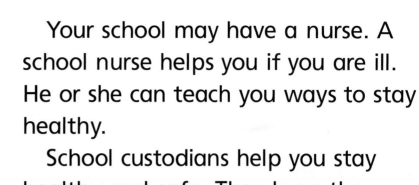

Your school may have a nurse. A school nurse helps you if you are ill. He or she can teach you ways to stay healthy.

School custodians help you stay healthy and safe. They keep the school clean.

You can help yourself stay healthy at school, too. Pick up your trash. Follow school rules that help everyone stay healthy and safe.

Review

1 How do people at school help you stay healthy and safe?

2 Where can you learn about being healthy?

3 Write about ways you can help keep your school clean and safe.

Community Helpers

Lesson Focus
Workers in your community help you stay safe and healthy.

Vocabulary
community

A **community** is a place where people live and work. Special community workers help people stay safe and healthy. Firefighters put out fires and rescue people. Police officers make sure people follow laws. Trash collectors keep the streets clean.

Emergency medical workers take hurt or very sick people to a hospital. At a hospital, people are helped by doctors and nurses.

At a library, you can learn about being healthy. Librarians help you and your family get good health information.

What places in this town have workers who help people stay safe and healthy?

You may need help if there is a fire, a car crash, or another emergency. Call 911 if you need help. The 911 operator can send the right people to help you.

Firefighters help you if a fire starts. They also rescue people hurt in car crashes.

Police officers come to your home if you do not feel safe. They help stop crime.

Emergency medical workers help people who are badly injured or ill. Then the workers take the ill or injured people to a hospital. Doctors, nurses, and other workers at the hospital also help the injured people.

Review

1. **Vocabulary** What is a **community**?

2. When should you call 911?

3. Write about three kinds of workers who help people in a community stay healthy and safe. Tell what they do.

Getting Rid of Trash

Getting rid of trash helps keep the land, air, and water clean. Trash that is left around may make people ill. Always throw trash into a trash can. Trash collectors will take the trash away to be burned or put into the ground.

You can also help make less trash. One way is to reuse things instead of throwing them away.

Recycling also helps make less trash. **Recycling** uses the materials in old things to make new things. Plastic, glass, metal, and paper can be recycled.

These bottles are made of plastic. They are recycled into material that is used to make the boardwalk.

Review

1. **Vocabulary** What is **recycling**? What materials can be recycled?

2. Name two ways you can make less trash.

3. Write about ways you can help get rid of trash at school.

Make Decisions

When you can choose from different things to do, you have to make a **decision**. What should you do with something after you have used it? Here is a way to make a good decision.

1 **Think about the choices.**

Mia thinks about her empty bottle. She can throw it onto the ground. She can reuse it. She can recycle it.

2 **Say NO to choices that are against the law or your family rules.**

Mia will not throw her bottle onto the ground. Littering is against the law and her family rules.

3 Ask yourself what could happen with each choice.

4 Make the best choice.

If Mia recycles, a truck will take away the bottle to be made into a new thing. If she reuses the bottle, she can drink from it later.

Mia decides to reuse her bottle. That way she can refill it with water to use when she is thirsty later.

Problem Solving

Use the steps to solve this problem.

You and your brother have finished eating some applesauce. Now you have the empty plastic jar. What should you do with it? How can you make a good decision?

Keeping Air and Water Clean

You need clean air and water to live and stay healthy. But air and water are not always clean. Dirt, germs, and other harmful things get into the air. This is called **air pollution**. Dirt, germs, and other things get into water, too. This is called **water pollution**.

People can help keep the air clean.
Smoke from the gas that cars burn
makes the air dirty. People can help by
riding bikes or walking when they can,
instead of driving cars.

People can help keep water clean,
too. Never throw trash into a lake,
pond, or ocean. Pick up your trash, and
put it into a trash can.

Air pollution can come from burning things. Dirty air harms your lungs. It makes it hard to breathe.

Dirty air and water can make people and animals ill. They also make it hard for plants to grow.

water cleaning facility

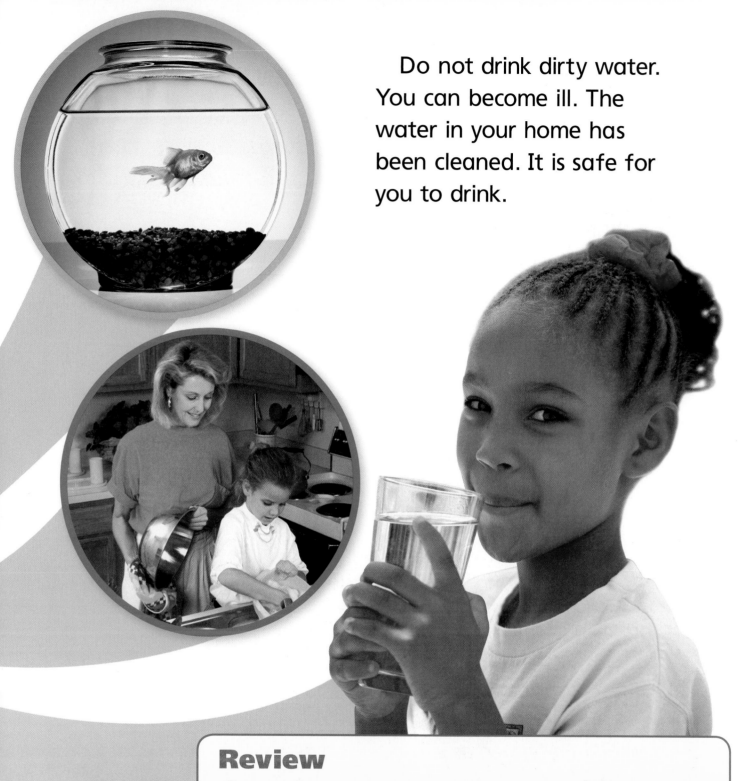

Do not drink dirty water. You can become ill. The water in your home has been cleaned. It is safe for you to drink.

Review

1 **Vocabulary** What causes **air pollution**?

2 How can people make less water pollution?

3 Write about why it is important to have clean air and water.

ACTIVITIES

Math

Tree Planting Graph

In what month were the most trees planted?

How many fewer trees were planted in March than in May?

Make your own graph about planting.

Writing

Invitation

Make a card to invite a community worker to speak at your school. You might ask a nurse, a firefighter, or a police officer.

 For more activities, visit The Learning Site.
www.harcourtschool.com/health

Citizenship

Being a Good Citizen at School

You help your school when you follow the safety rules. You can also help by picking up your trash. You can raise money for groups that help people who are ill or in need. You can help others choose healthful lunches.

Helping at school shows that you are a good **citizen**. You are a helpful member of your school and community.

How are these children being good citizens?

Activity

With a group, write a plan to make your school safer and more healthful.

Use Health Words

Use the words to tell about the pictures.

1 community

2 recycling

3 air pollution

4 water pollution

(Focus Skill) Reading Skill

5 Tell some causes for this effect.

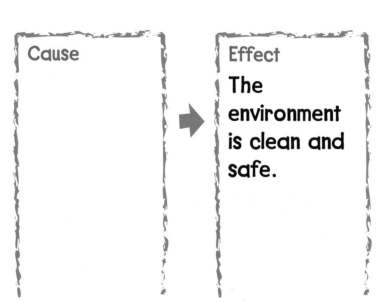

Cause	Effect
	The environment is clean and safe.

Use Life Skills

Look at the pictures. Then answer the questions.

a.

b.

6 Which picture shows Mia after she has made her choice?

7 What are four steps you can use to make choices?

Write About It

8 How do community workers help you stay healthy?

A doctor gives me check-ups.

Find Cause and Effect

Learning how to find cause and effect can help you understand what you read. You can use a chart like this to help you find cause and effect.

Cause	Effect
A cause is why something happens.	An effect is what happens.

Some paragraphs have more than one cause or effect. Read this paragraph.

Kathy eats many kinds of healthful foods. She visits her doctor for regular checkups. Kathy stays healthy and strong.

This chart shows two causes and their effect in the paragraph.

Cause	Effect
Kathy eats many kinds of healthful foods. Kathy visits her doctor for regular checkups.	Kathy stays healthy and strong.

Find the Main Idea

Learning how to find the main idea can help you understand what you read. The main idea of a paragraph is what it is mostly about. The details tell you more about it.

Read this paragraph.

> Amy follows safety rules about fire. She wants to light a candle. She knows that she should never play with matches or lighters. She asks her grandma to help her.

This chart shows the main idea and details.

Detail
Amy wants to light a candle.

Detail
She does not use a lighter.

Main Idea
Amy follows safety rules about fire.

Detail
She does not use matches.

Detail
Amy asks her grandma for help.

Make Predictions

Focus Skill

Learning how to make predictions can help you understand what you read. A prediction is what you think will happen next.

Some paragraphs give clues that help you predict what will happen next.

Diego has been taking good care of his body. He gets plenty of sleep. He eats healthful food. He runs and plays every day. Diego is visiting the doctor today for a checkup.

This chart shows the prediction made from the clues in the paragraph.

Prediction
I think Diego will have a good checkup.

What Happened
The doctor said Diego was strong and healthy.

⭐ Recall and Retell

Learning how to recall and retell details can help you understand what you read. Some sentences tell the main idea. Some sentences tell details.

Read this paragraph.

> Janie was worried that she would not have friends in her new neighborhood. She felt lonely. Janie talked to her mom about her problem. This made her feel better.

This chart shows how to recall and retell what the paragraph is about.

	Retell
Recall Detail Janie was worried that she would not make friends.	Janie's mom helped her feel better about not having friends in her new neighborhood.
Recall Detail Janie felt lonely.	
Recall Detail Janie talked to her mom about her problem.	

Sequence

Learning how to find sequence can help you understand what you read. You can use a chart like this to help you find sequence.

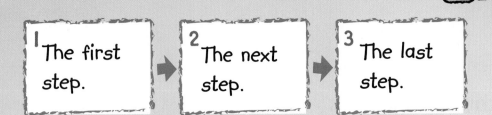

1 The first step. → 2 The next step. → 3 The last step.

Some paragraphs use words that help you understand order. Read this paragraph. Look at the underlined words.

To be safe, do not talk to strangers. <u>First</u>, walk away quickly. <u>Next</u>, tell an adult. <u>Last</u>, if you need help, call 911 to tell the police.

This chart shows the sequence of the paragraph.

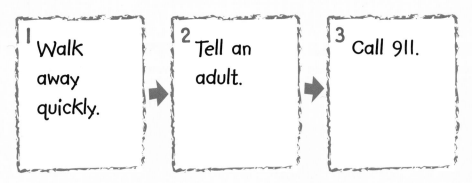

1 Walk away quickly. → 2 Tell an adult. → 3 Call 911.

Use Context Clues

Learning how to use context clues can help you understand what you read. Context clues are words or pictures near a word. You can use a chart to help you use context clues.

Some paragraphs use words that may be new to you. Read this paragraph. Look for clues that can help you find the meaning of the underlined word.

Greg wants to eat the right kinds of food to keep his teeth healthy. He knows he needs foods with the mineral called <u>calcium</u>. He will drink milk and eat cheese and yogurt.

This chart shows the context clues in the paragraph.

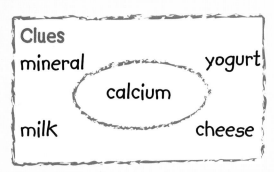

Health and Safety

First Aid for Kids

You can help someone who is hurt and stay safe, too. You will need to know these things.

Know when to call 911.

Know how the body works.

Know how to check for safety.

Know how to prevent injury.

Earthquake Safety Tips

- If you are outside, stay there. Move away from buildings and electric wires.

- If you are inside, go under a doorway or a heavy table or desk. Stay away from glass doors and windows.

- After the earthquake there may be aftershocks. Watch for falling objects.

Storm Safety Tips

In a Tornado

Go to a safe area away from doors and windows. A hallway or basement is best.

In a Hurricane

Stay in a room in the middle of the house. Listen to weather reports for what to do.

Stranger Danger

Be safe. Follow these rules.

- Never talk to strangers.

- Never go anywhere with a stranger.

- Do not open the door if you are home alone.

- Do not tell anyone on the telephone that you are home alone unless you are calling 911.

- Do not give your name, address, or telephone number to a stranger.

- If you are lost, tell a police officer, a guard, or a store clerk.

Prevent Poisoning

A poison is something that can kill you or make you very ill. Some poisons have special uses. Only adults can use them safely.

These pictures mark a poison.

Keep Away from Poisons

- Know the pictures and words that mark poisons.

- Never take any medicines or vitamins by yourself. Always ask an adult to help you.

- Never use cleaning products by yourself. Never mix cleaning products.

- Never use insect sprays or lotions by yourself. Always ask an adult to help you.

My Internet Safety Rules

1. I will never give anyone my name or address unless my parents know about it.

2. I will tell my parents if I see something that does not seem right for me to see.

3. I will never agree to get together with someone I meet online.

4. I will talk with my parents about rules for going online. I will follow those rules.

Family Emergency Plan

Your family can be safe in an emergency by following a plan.

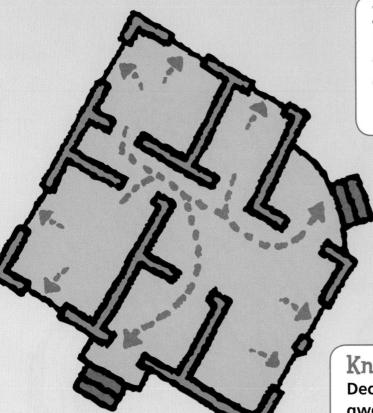

Have Two Meeting Places

Decide on two places to meet. One should be about a block away and the other at least a mile away.

Know What Could Happen

Learn what emergencies might happen in your area.

Know Your Family Contact

Decide on someone who lives far away to be a contact person. Know the person's name, address, and telephone number.

Have Emergency Drills

Practice getting out of your home safely.

Make an Emergency Kit

Gather first-aid items, food, and water.

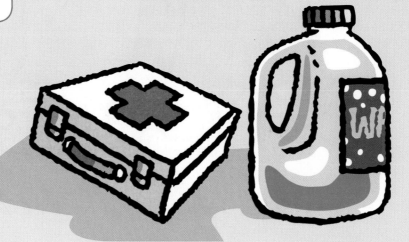

Backpack Safety

Carrying a backpack that is too heavy can injure your back. Carrying one the wrong way can also hurt you.

Right way   **Wrong way**

Glossary

ad (AD): A message that tries to get people to buy a product (40)

air pollution (AIR puh•LOO•shuhn): Harmful things in the air that make it unsafe to breathe (240)

alcohol (AL•kuh•hawl): A drug found in beer, wine, and liquor (178)

allergy (AL•er•jee): An illness that causes a person not to feel well after eating a certain food or touching or being near a certain plant or animal (156)

asthma (AZ•muh): An illness that does not spread and that makes it hard to breathe (158)

balanced diet (BAL•uhnst DY•uht): A diet, or meal plan, with the right amounts of foods from each food group (74)

blood vessels (BLUHD VEH•suhlz): Tubes that carry blood from the heart to every part of the body (14)

brain (BRAYN): The part of the nervous system that gets information from the five senses, controls all parts of the body, and lets a person think and remember (16)

caffeine (ka•FEEN): A legal drug found in coffee, tea, chocolate, and some soft drinks (174)

caring (KAIR•ing): Kind and thoughtful (21, 163)

cavity (KA•vuh•tee): A hole in a tooth (51)

chores (CHAWRZ): Jobs a family member is responsible for doing to help the family (214)

circulatory system (SER•kyuh•luh•tawr•ee SIS•tuhm): The heart and blood vessels, which work together to pump and carry blood through the body (14)

citizen (SIH•tuh•zuhn): A member of a community (245)

citizenship (SIH•tuh•zuhn•ship): The way a person acts to be a good citizen, or member, of a community (143)

communicate (kuh•MYOO•nih•kayt): To talk to and listen to another person (36, 150)

community (kuh•MYOO•nih•tee): A place where people live and work (232)

conflict (KAHN•flikt): A disagreement or argument (132, 218)

decision (dih•SIH•zhun): A choice a person makes (80, 238)

dental hygienist (DENT•uhl hy•JEN•ist): A person who works with a dentist; he or she cleans teeth and makes sure people know how to take care of their teeth (58)

digestive system (dy•JES•tuhv SIS•tuhm): The mouth, stomach, intestines, and other parts of the body that help the body use food to get energy (10)

disease (dih•ZEEZ): A kind of illness (152)

divorce (dih•VAWRS): A change in a family that happens when a mother and father or two other adults are not married anymore (222)

drugs (DRUHGZ): Things other than food that change the way the body works (172)

emotions (ih•MOH•shuhnz): Feelings (195)

energy (EN•er•jee): The power the body needs to do things (66)

exercise (EK•ser•syz): Activity that makes the body work hard (90)

fair (FAIR): Treating everyone in the same way; truthful about what happens (225)

fairness (FAIR•nuhs): Equal treatment of everyone (103)

fat (FAT): A part of food that gives the body energy (73)

fire drills (FYR DRILZ): Practices for getting out of a building safely if it is on fire (110)

fit (FIT): Healthy and having lots of energy (90)

floss (FLAHS): A kind of thread used to clean between teeth (54)

germs (JERMZ): Tiny things that can make a person ill (28, 152)

goal (GOHL): Something to work toward (18, 56)

growing (GROH•ing): Getting bigger and older (4)

habit (HAB•it): An action that a person does often (175)

head lice (HED LYS): Tiny insects that live in the hair and are easily spread from person to person (30)

heart (HART): The muscle that pumps, or pushes, blood through blood vessels (14)

helmet (HEL•muht): A hard, padded head covering that protects the skull and brain (135)

honest (AH•nihst): Truthful (61)

honesty (AH•nihs•tee): Truthfulness (85)

ill (IL): Not well; sick (148)

ingredients (in•GREE•dee•uhnts): The things a food is made from (75)

injury (IN•jer•ee): Hurt or harm to the body (136)

intestines (in•TES•tuhnz): The part of the digestive system through which food passes after it leaves the stomach (10)

label (LAY•buhl): Words on a package that list what is in the product and tell what the product does (38)

love (LUHV): A special feeling of caring for someone (212)

lungs (LUHNGZ): The parts of the respiratory system that take in oxygen from air (13)

meal (MEEL): The food that is eaten at a certain time each day (72)

mouth (MOWTH): The part of the digestive system that takes in food (11)

muscles (MUH•suhlz): Body parts that support the body and help it move (8)

muscular system (MUHS•kyuh•ler SIS•tuhm): All the muscles of the body (8)

MyPyramid (MY PIH•ruh•mid): A diagram that shows the food groups that foods belong to and how much food from each group to eat (69)

needs (NEEDZ): Things that a person must have to live (194)

nervous system (NER•vuhs SIS•tuhm): The brain and the nerves, which work together to control the body (16)

nicotine (NIH•kuh•teen): A harmful drug found in tobacco (176)

911 (NYN WUHN WUHN): The phone number to call in an emergency (111)

over-the-counter medicines (OH•ver thuh KOWN•ter MEH•dih•suhnz): Medicines that adults can buy without a doctor's order (171)

passenger (PAS•uhn•jer): A person who rides in a car, bus, or other vehicle (138)

permanent teeth (PER•muh•nuhnt TEETH): The second set of teeth, which grow in after the primary teeth fall out (49)

poisons (POY•zuhnz): Things that can hurt or even kill a person if they get inside the body (114)

prescription medicines (prih•SKRIP•shun MEH•dih•suhnz): Medicines that a doctor orders for a person (170)

primary teeth (PRY•mair•ee TEETH): Baby teeth; the first set of teeth a person gets (49)

recycling (ree•SY•kling): Using the materials in old things to make new things (237)

refuse (rih•FYOOZ): To say NO to something (118, 182)

resolve (rih•ZAHLV): To settle, or end, a conflict (132, 218)

respect (rih•SPEKT): Thoughtfulness and politeness in what is said and done (43, 202, 207)

respiratory system (RES•per•uh•tawr•ee SIS•tuhm): The parts of the body, including the mouth, nose, and lungs, that allow a person to breathe (12)

responsibility (rih•SPAHN•suh•BIHL•uh•tee): The ability to do the right things (185)

responsible (rih•SPAHN•suh•buhl): Able to be trusted to do the right things (121, 200)

rules (ROOLZ): Directions or laws that tell what to do and what not to do (98)

safety (SAYF•tee): Being safe from danger; not getting hurt (96)

safety belt (SAYF•tee BELT): A strap that holds a passenger safely in a seat (138)

safety gear (SAYF•tee GEER): Clothing and equipment such as helmets, knee pads, elbow pads, and wrist guards worn to protect the body from injury (136)

self-control (SELF kuhn•TROHL): Control of one's own actions and emotions (181, 197)

skeletal system (SKEL•uh•tuhl SIS•tuhm): The skeleton; all of the bones, which hold up the body and protect soft body parts (6)

skull (SKUHL): The bones of the head and face (7)

special (SPEH•shuhl): Different from all others (190)

spine (SPYN): The backbone; the bones of the neck and back (7)

stomach (STUH•muhk): The part of the digestive system in which food is mixed with juices to become a thick liquid (11)

strangers (STRAYN•jerz): People a person does not know well (116)

stress (STRES): Feelings of worry, nervousness, or excitement (94, 198)

sunburn (SUHN•bern): A burning of the skin caused by the sun's rays (26)

sunscreen (SUHN•skreen): A lotion or cream that protects the skin from the sun (27)

teeth (TEETH): The parts of the digestive system used to bite and chew food (11)

tobacco (tuh•BA•koh): A plant that contains nicotine and other drugs; it is smoked in cigarettes, cigars, and pipes and may also be chewed (176)

tobacco smoke (tuh•BA•koh SMOHK): Smoke from tobacco, which contains drugs and is harmful to people who breathe it (177)

tongue (TUHNG): The part of the digestive system that lets a person taste and swallow food (11)

vaccine (vak•SEEN): A medicine, usually given in a shot, that can protect a person from a certain disease (155)

wants (WAHNTS): Things that a person would like to have but does not need (194)

wastes (WAYSTS): Things that the body does not need (71)

water pollution (WAW•ter puh•LOO•shuhn): Harmful things in the water that make it unsafe to use (240)

weapons (WEP•uhnz): Things such as guns and knives that can be used to hurt a person (112)

Index

Boldfaced numbers refer to illustrations.

Checkup
dentist, 58–59, **58–59**, 160–161
doctor, 155, 160–161
hearing test, **34**, 35
at school, 155
vision test, 33, **33**
Chewing food, 10–11, **10–11**, 48
Chicken pox, 155
Choking, 131, **131**
Choosing
foods, 68–81, **68–69**, **72–75**, 84, **84**
products, 39, **39**
things to do, 238–239, **238–239**, 247, **247**
Chores, 200, **200**, 214–215, **214**, 224, **224**
Cigarettes. See Tobacco
Circulatory system, 14–15, **14–15**
Citizen, 245
Citizenship, xiv, **xiv**, 143, **143**, 245, **245**
Cleanliness
of air and water, 240–243, **240–243**
with animal bites and scratches, 129, **129**
of ears, 35
of skin, 28, **28**
of teeth, 52–53, **52–53**
and wellness, 161
Clues, context, 47, **47**, 62, **62**, 167, **167**, 186, **186**, 253, **253**
Colds, 152, 157
Communicate, xii, **xii**, 36–37, **36–37**, 45, **45**, 150–151, **150–151**, 165, **165**
Community, 232, **232–233**
Community helpers, 33. **33–34**, 35, 58–59, **58–59**, 61–63, 113, 126, 149, **155**, 161, 170–171, **170**, **179**, 181, **181**, 232–236, **232–235**, 244, 247
Computers, and Internet
safety, **24**, **231**, 260, **260**
using, 20, 42, 60, 84, 102, 120, 142, 162, 184, 206, 224, 230–232, **231**, 244
Conflict, 132, 218
Conflict resolution, xiii, **xiii**, 132–133, **132–133**, 145, 145, 218–219, **218–219**, 227, **227**
Consumer influences. See Ads; Influences on buying decisions; Labels
Context clues, 47, **47**, 62, **62**, 167, **167**, 186, **186**, 253, **253**
Cooling down, 97
Coping strategies. See Life Skills
Coughing, 150, **150**, 152–153
Crossing guard, 113, **113**, 134, **134**
Custodian, school, 231

D

Daily Physical Activity, 3, 25, 47, 65, 89, 107, 125, 147, 167, 189, 211, 229
Danger, avoiding, 106–123
fires, 108–111, **108–109**, 111
poisons, 114–115, **114–115**, 259
with strangers, 116–117, **116–117**, 258
weapons, 112–113, **112–113**
Dangerous substances, avoiding. See Danger, avoiding; Drugs, Poisons

Death, of family member or pet, 220, **220**
Decision, 80, 238
Decision making, xii, **xii**
choosing products, 39, **39**
choosing snacks, 51, **51**, 80–81, **80–81**, 87, **87**
choosing the right thing to do, 160, 238–239, **238–239**, 247, **247**
Dental hygienist, 58, **58**, 63
Dentist, 58–59, **59**, 61, 63, 161
Diaphragm, 12
Diet, balanced, 74. See also Foods
Digestive system, 10–11, **10–11**
Dinner, 72, **73**
Disease, 152. See also Illness
Divorce, 222, **222**
Doctor, 33. **33–34**, 35, 61–63, 129, 149, 170–171, 233, 235, **235**
Drugs, 172–185, **172**, **174**, **176–177**, **179**
ads for, 180, **180**
alcohol, 172, **172**, 178–179, **178–179**
caffeine, 172, **172**, 174–175, **174**, 184
saying NO to, 173, 180–183, **182–183**, 187, **187**
tobacco, 172, **172**, 176–177, **176–177**, 182–183, **182–183**
See also Medicines

E

Ears
caring for, 35, **35**
inside of, 34, **34**
outside of, 34, **34**
protecting, 35, **35**
Earthquake safety, 110. 130, 257
Elbow pads, 7, 90, 98–99, **99**, 136
Emergencies, 234–235, **234–235**, 261
Emergency medical workers, **179**, 233, **233**, 235, 235
Emergency plan, family, 261
Emotions, 195. See also Feelings
Energy, and foods, 66–67, **66–67**, 72
Equipment, protective. See Safety; Safety gear; Safety pads; Safety rules
and bones, 7
cooling down from, 97, **97**
and heart muscle, 15, **15**
and lungs, 13, **13**
and muscles, 9, **9**, **96**
planning for, 18–19, **18–19**, 102, **102**
protection during, 98–99, **99**. See also Safety gear
rules for, 98
and safety, 96–99, **96–99**
setting goals for, 18–19, **18–19**
tally table for, 20, **20**
warming up for, 96, **96**
and wellness, 160–161, **161**
Eyes
caring for, 33, **33**
inside of, 32, **32**
outside of, 32, **32**
protecting, 33, **33**, 99, 154

273

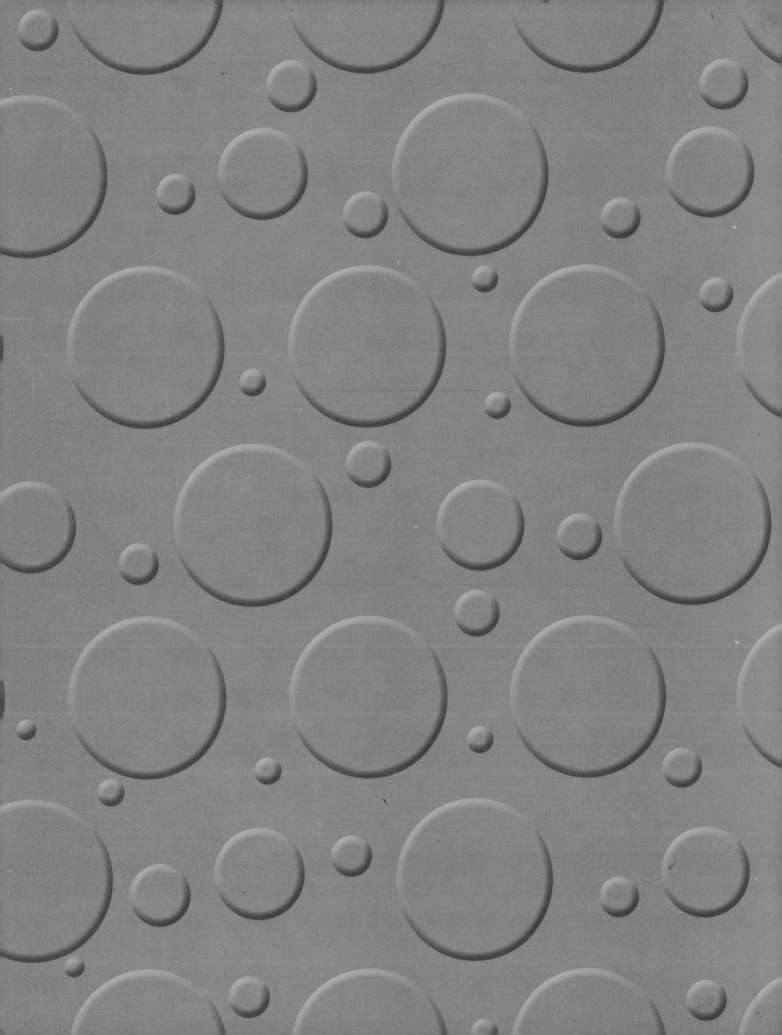